THE WRITING OF

AMERICAN

MILITARY HISTORY

A Guide

This pamphlet supersedes DA Pam 20-200, 9 August 1951

DEPARTMENT OF THE ARMY
WASHINGTON 25, D. C., *24 August 1956*

DA Pamphlet 20-200 is published for the information and guidance of all concerned.

[AG 314.7 (6 Apr 56)]

By Order of *Wilber M. Brucker,* Secretary of the Army:

MAXWELL D. TAYLOR,
General, United States Army,
Chief of Staff.

Official:
JOHN A. KLEIN,
Major General, United States Army,
The Adjutant General.

Distribution:
Active Army:

Gen Staff, DA (5)
SS, DA (5)
CMH (200)
Tec Svc, DA (5)
Admin & Tec Svc Bd (1)
Hq CONARC (25)
OS Maj Comd (10)
MDW (1)

Armies (5)
Corps (3)
Div (1)
ICAF (40)
NWC (60)
Gen & Br Svc Sch (5)
PMST (1)
Mil Dist (1)

NG: State AG (1); Div (1).
USAR: Div (1).
For explanation of abbreviations used, see SR 320-50-1.

For sale by the Superintendent of Documents, U. S. Government Printing Office
Washington 25, D. C. — Price $1.50

FOREWORD

The Writing of American Military History: A Guide, should stimulate intelligent probing into the past with an eye to the future. This, in turn, should lead to increased wisdom and, therefore, to wiser decisions and better execution throughout the Army in peace and war.

All officers of the United States Army, but particularly those having historical assignments and undergoing instruction at the service schools and colleges or civilian educational institutions, will find the text helpful. Scholars and others interested in American military affairs may also find it very useful.

PREFACE

The need for guidance in historical study and research has existed in the United States Army for a very long time. Various attempts have been made, from time to time, to fill that need. For the most part this was accomplished by issuing suggested courses of historical study and by publishing pamphlets on methodology at the various service schools and colleges. The reading lists were not scientifically arranged and led to aimless historical study. The methodologies were not systematized and thus precluded the early acquisition of a method of research that could be utilized continuously throughout an officer's service.

The primary purpose of this text is to bring order out of chaos in the fields of historical study and research in the United States Army. In line with the views of Clausewitz, the principal object of the text is to stimulate a progressive and scientific study of United States military history and leadership with the hope that it will "produce searching rather than inventive minds and cool rather than hot heads," [1] to which the safety of our country can be most advantageously entrusted in time of emergency or war. In commenting upon this objective, General of the Army George C. Marshall wrote that: "If you can stimulate by your list, a desire for wide reading among officers to supplement their professional experience, you will have performed a fine service."

The secondary object of the text is to clarify what is meant by a military historian. A military historian is one who is well-informed in military history and in subjects related to the military profession. Therefore, *any professionally qualified officer is a military historian.* In a narrower sense, a military historian is a writer or chronicler of military activities. It necessarily follows that the influence of a military man upon history can be extended beyond the field of action into that of theory or historical works dealing with the art and science of war.

In a real sense an officer's value to the military service, especially in high-level positions, may be determined to a considerable degree by his qualifications as a military historian. It is important, therefore, that professional military men should assiduously study military history throughout their service. They also should strive to acquire skill in historical research and a lucid and logical style of presenting historical accounts of military operations and activities. But more important still, they should develop proficiency in evaluating historical events and in analyzing them with a view of determining the lessons that can be learned from the past.

Special thanks are due the Library of Congress and the National Archives for their assistance in preparing the text.

[1] Carl von Clausewitz, *On War*, trans. J. J. Graham (London, 1940), I, p. 71.

CONTENTS

CHAPTER I
INTRODUCTION

General

The value of history in military education has always been recognized in the United States Army as in most armies. It has been at the very base of instruction in the service academy, schools, and colleges since their inception. In this emphasis on the value of history in military instruction, the American Army has followed the advice of such great captains as Frederick the Great and Napoleon, as well as others who have more recently made their mark on the pages of history. Napoleon has written, ". . . the knowledge of the higher arts of war is not acquired except by experience and the study of history of wars and the battles of great captains." [1] Gen. George S. Patton, Jr., one of America's great offensive battle leaders, also emphasized the importance of history. His words, written on the battlefield, were: "To be a successful soldier you must know history, read it objectively—dates and even minute details of tactics are useless. . . . You must [also] read biography and especially autobiography. If you will do it you will find war is simple." [2]

There are dissenters from this point of view, however. Field Marshal Wavell, for one, holds that psychology and leadership are of greater importance to a military man than the study of operations, contending that Napoleon's military success can be attributed to his knowledge of psychology rather than to his study of tactics and strategy. [3] And Le Bon, who was not a military man, has condemned histories on general principle, observing that "They are fanciful accounts of ill-observed facts accompanied by explanations the result of reflection" and that the writing "of such books is a most absolute waste of time." [4]

Notwithstanding these opinions, which are not without value as a challenge to historians, it must be concluded that the study of past wars is fundamental to preparation for the next, for current military problems cannot be solved without an understanding of the past from which they stem. Every individual in the military service will

---

[1] Napoleon, *Memoires ecrits a Sainte-Hélène*, ed. Gaspard Gourgand (London, 1823), II, p. 51.

[2] Harry H. Semmes, "A Portrait of Patton." MS in author's files.

[3] Earl Wavell, *The Good Soldier* (London, 1948), pp. 20–21.

[4] Le Bon, *The Crowd* (London, 1921), p. 54.

find a knowledge of military history, and especially of American military history, valuable in the solution of problems, both in peace and in war. Heeding the inscription carved in stone at the entrance to the National Archives—"What is past is prologue"—the soldier must be rooted in the past to understand the present that he may project himself into the future.

Military History in the Development of Esprit de Corps and Morale

Esprit de Corps

Clausewitz has said: "One who is seeking a profound understanding of the fundamentals of war must understand *esprit de corps*. This spirit is the cement which binds together all qualities which taken together give an army military value." Although "order, skill, a certain pride, and high morale are highly prized peacetime qualities, . . . they provide no spur to excellence or sacrifice." A capable commander is required to lead such an army "with the utmost of care, until, gradually, victory and exertion give it real strength, real fighting spirit."[5]

At the very base of this fighting spirit is patriotism or love of country—the cement that binds a people together and assists their fighting men. Without it neither the people nor the Army has a soul. The founders of the Republic laid a solid spiritual foundation for all Americans in two great documents—*The Declaration of Independence* and *The Constitution*. In these fundamental papers are recorded the ideas and principles upon which patriotism in the United States must be built. Accordingly, every man who enters the military service must swear or affirm that he will defend the *Constitution* against all enemies, foreign or domestic. This solemn ceremony is surrounded with all the pomp and circumstance possible under prevailing conditions.

In writing about patriotism Gen. Ian Hamilton of Great Britain said that "It is a plant whose best nutriments are blood and tears: a plant which dies down in peace and flowers most brightly in war. It does not calculate, does not profiteer, does not stop to reason: in an atmosphere of danger the sap begins to stir, it lives, it takes possession of the soul."[6] A truly great military historian will attempt to capture and record this spirit which plays such an important role in the outcome of battles, campaigns, and wars. A mere recitation of events will fail to probe the depths of the services and will prove of little value to leaders of men.

---

[5] Clausewitz, *On War*, vol. III, ch. 5.
[6] Sir Ian Hamilton, *The Soul and Body of an Army* (London, 1921), p. 214.

2

The accomplishments of the United States Army in both peace and war have been so outstanding that every soldier can gain inspiration from the record of the past even though still imperfectly told. During the comparatively short span of American history, the Army has fought brave and skillful soldiers of many races and in many lands. These operations have ranged from desperate hand-to-hand engagements with savages equipped with bows and arrows and tomahawks or spears and bolos to vast battles with armies landing in the face of modern forces and driving them back to the center of empire. The Army has also played an outstanding role in discovery and exploration; in great engineering undertakings that have joined the oceans, developed ports and harbors, harnessed and controlled rivers, and developed the atomic bombs; in medicine and hygiene; and in communications and aviation. It has also been the training ground of scholars, scientists, administrators, educators, diplomats, and statesmen who have made great contributions to every phase of American life.

A knowledge of its accomplishments can play a vital role in the development of *esprit de corps* in the Army, for as the eminent British military historian Fortescue has said, "Without knowledge of military history men are really unconscious of the existence of the most wonderful of moral forces . . . ; and it is not a thing of which anyone can afford to be ignorant." [7] In line with Fortescue's warning the United States Army has used military history in many ways.[8] In the Education and Information program, the soldiers are informed of past heroic deeds and accomplishments of individuals and units and are furnished *The Soldier's Guide,* containing historical material. In many units mounts and vehicles have borne the names of distinguished soldiers of the past. Army posts are generally named for widely known military men; buildings and streets for others or for military organizations. Colors and standards are decorated with streamers carrying the names of battles or campaigns in which the unit has honorably participated. For many years *Retreat* has included *The Star Spangled Banner* which was inspired under the "rocket's red glare." Such things can be turned to advantage by those who will take the trouble to weld the deeds and records of the past to the task in hand and, if successfully accomplished, the Army-in-being will live and function in the best traditions of the past.

Morale

Morale may be defined as the discipline and spirit which pervades an army or people. In speaking on morale Gen. George C. Marshall, Chief of Staff, United States Army, once said:

---

[7] J. W. Fortescue, *A Military History* (Cambridge, 1914), p. 39.
[8] DA Cir 100, "Military History Indoctrination Plan," 1952.

The soldier's heart, the soldier's spirit, the soldier's soul, are everything. Unless the soldier's soul sustains him he cannot be relied on and will fail himself and his commander and his country in the end.

It is not enough to fight. It is the spirit which we bring to the fight that decides the issue. It is morale that wins the victory.

Morale is the state of mind. It is steadfastness and courage and hope. It is confidence and zeal and loyalty. It is *elan, esprit de corps* and determination.

It is staying power, the spirit which endures to the end—the will to win.

With it all things are possible, without it everything else, planning, preparation, production, count for naught.[9]

As can be seen General Marshall's thoughts were of the spiritual attributes that motivate individuals, who collectively make up a unit and the entire Army.

Gen. William T. Sherman has given his views on the importance of the spiritual side of the Army in these words: "There is a soul to an army as well as to individual men, and no general can accomplish the full work of his army unless he commands the soul of his men, as well as their bodies and legs."[10] General Patton, a profound student of military history and leadership, on many occasions during World War II also noted the unit soul, physically symbolized by the colors and standards.

It can thus be seen that both Sherman and Patton broadened the concept to include the unit as well as the individual in the broader problems of morale. They thought of the individuals of a unit welded together by a leader and given a common soul. The creation of this unit soul is the continuing problem of all commanders from the lowest to the highest and the problem becomes more difficult when, for reasons of economy, the props which support a commander are abolished. But, regardless of handicaps, the quality of a leader is the true criterion of the soul of a unit. He is the one who must inspire the individuals of the outfit and weld them into a whole capable of withstanding all hardships and sacrifices so well illustrated by Capt. Nathan Hale as he stood on the enemy's gallows on the morning of 22 September 1776 and said: "I only regret that I have but one life to lose for my country."

Role of Symbols in Developing Morale

Intangible Symbols

Intangible symbols of the unit's past consist of customs and traditions around which the outfit builds distinctive special observances

---

[9] *Selected Speeches and Statements of General of the Army George C. Marshall*, ed. H. A. DeWeerd (Washington, 1945), pp. 121–25.

[10] William T. Sherman, *Personal Memoirs of Gen. W. T. Sherman* (New York, 1875), III, p. 387.

and practices. Such things can be of considerable morale value in the Army. Examples of these are almost endless in number and variety. Some of the most widely practiced are the celebration of important unit anniversaries, minor distinctions of drill and command, and distinctive greetings and replies. For example, an individual of the 13th Cavalry on receiving an order or instructions used to salute and reply before departing, "It shall be done." The 7th Cavalry once included saddled but riderless Comanche, the lone survivor of the Battle of the Little Big Horn, in its parades. In 1922 the 3d Infantry was granted permission to march on all ceremonial occasions with fixed bayonets in honor of its gallant assault with the bayonet at the battle of Cerro Gordo on 18 April 1847.

Commodore Oliver Hazard Perry, a naval hero beloved by the Army, knew the value of symbolism and history. After building a fleet on Lake Erie during the War of 1812, he named his flagship for an earlier hero, Capt. James Lawrence, and put out a blue, bunting flag carrying Lawrence's last words, "Don't give up the ship!" With a crew of soldiers and sailors he defeated the British fleet and sent a laconic message to Maj. Gen. William H. Harrison, "We have met the enemy and they are ours." Then after transporting Harrison's force across Lake Erie, he joined it ashore and participated in a cavalry charge that clinched an important American victory in the Battle of the Thames.[11] The Army has named a camp in Ohio in memory of Perry. The Navy has named a ship for him and all entering midshipmen at the United States Naval Academy are sworn in and take the oath of allegiance directly beneath his flag, which is on permanent display in Memorial Hall.

Lt. Gen. Winfield Scott was a colorful leader with ability to express himself in words that have become the heritage of units that once served under his command. After the fall of Chapultepec, 13 September 1847, the 3d Infantry Regiment was put at the head of the column making formal entrance into Mexico City. Mounted with his staff, General Scott waited for the procession in the outskirts. When the 3d Infantry came abreast, Scott, in a dramatic gesture, swept off his hat and said to his staff, "Gentlemen, take off your hats to the Old Guard." This nickname has persisted and is in use today. On the same occasion he addressed the Regiment of Mounted Rifles as follows, "Brave Rifles! Veterans! You have been baptised in fire and blood and come out steel." Since that time the regiment has proudly called itself "Brave Rifles" and its unit insignia is emblazoned with that name.

The 13th Infantry earned a special name as a result of the gallantry displayed by the 1st Battalion at Vicksburg on 19 May 1863.

---

[11] Commodore Dudley W. Knox, *A History of the United States Navy* (New York, 1948), pp. 114–19.

5

In a frontal assault the 13th planted and maintained its colors on the Confederate parapet for as long as the attack persisted. In doing so it lost 43.3 percent of its men. On 12 August 1863, a board of officers of the XV Corps authorized the regiment to inscribe "First at Vicksburg" upon its colors.

The 19th Infantry has for its motto, "Rock of Chickamauga." It earned this name while serving in the corps commanded by Maj. Gen. George H. Thomas in the Battle of Chickamauga. Stationed on the left of General Thomas' line on 19 September, the regiment bore the brunt of the fiercest assaults. The next day, when their ammunition was exhausted, the men held their ground with bayonets. Seventy-five percent of the regiment were killed or wounded. At the end of the battle a second lieutenant was in command. To commemorate this incident, it later became the custom for the junior second lieutenant of the 19th Infantry to command the regiment on Organization Day, 20 September.

Another example originated with the proud remark of an unknown soldier during the Civil War. During that war certain corps had adopted distinctive badges, a custom which has continued in the United States Army. But the XV Corps, commanded by Maj. Gen. John A. Logan, had not done so. One of the men of the corps, on being asked what his badge was, replied, "Forty rounds in the cartridge-box, and twenty in the pocket!" On hearing the story General Logan promptly adopted the cartridge-box and forty rounds as the corps-badge.[12]

Unit marches and songs are very effective intangible symbols, particularly when they have been associated with an outfit for a long time. Most of the older regiments have these songs or marches. The 7th Cavalry's *Garry Owen* is an example of a song that has contributed materially to the morale of that regiment for many years. Perhaps the most famous of the branch songs is Lt. Edmund L. Gruber's *The Caisson Song.* In a much more important way, however, *The Star Spangled Banner* has played an outstanding role in developing morale in the armed forces since it appeared during the War of 1812.

Many traditions and customs of the service have developed around the hallowed bugle calls that for years have clocked off the soldiers' hours from *First Call* for *Reveille* to *Taps.* Each call has a history of its own and frequently an accompanying song—some humorous, others sad. None is more interesting than *Taps,* the most beautiful of them all. Conceived by Brig. Gen. Daniel Butterfield during the Peninsular Campaign of the Civil War, *Taps* soon became the call to bed and finally took its place at the very end of the last rites paid to deceased service personnel. Through the

---

[12] Sherman, *op. cit.,* I, p. 391.

years, since its inception, the nostalgic, sad rhythm of this call has touched the hearts of all who have served their country.

Tangible Symbols

Colors and standards, campaign streamers, streamers for unit awards or citations, organizational and personal flags, guidons, silver bands, branch insignia, distinctive colors and buttons on uniforms, distinctive items of uniform, organizational shoulder patches, distinctive unit insignia, and insignia and chevrons of rank have all played an important role in the development of individual, unit, branch, and Army-wide pride of service. Because of their connection with the past these tangible symbols, so important in the development of morale and *esprit de corps* in the Army, should always be treated with special care and modified only when it is absolutely necessary to do so.

Role of Unit History in Developing Morale

The color-bearing units are the military families within which the broader soul of the Army is built. It is these families which the division commander, without infringing upon subordinates, welds into a composite team. These units are corporate entities having a legal existence even though their actual personnel may vary from war strength when on active service to zero when on an inactive status. Therefore, every organization has its own history which is distinct from all others. It may have a history extending back before the founding of the Republic, a brief history, or, in the case of new units, no history at all. In any case, however, each unit shares the history of the United States Army. Therefore, any commander can utilize history to teach pride in the unit's or Army's past accomplishments and to foster soldierly conduct, morale, and love of country. Newer outfits, like younger brothers, should strive to excel their seniors.

Military Memoirs and Biography and Leadership

Leadership being the very foundation upon which morale, *esprit de corps,* and a successful military career must be built, it behooves all officers to study it assiduously, for as Maj. Gen. Freytag-Loringhoven in his book, *The Power of Personality in War,* has said, "There is no profession in which personality training is more important than the military." The study can best be undertaken by gaining an understanding of the general principles of leadership and then by critically reading the memoirs and biographies of American military leaders with a view to determining the reasons for their successes and failures. The study of foreign military leaders is less important because the political and military institutions and the customs and traditions of other countries are different from those of the United States. It should be understood, however, that the qualities and methods of each individual are unique to himself and are not entirely suited to any other. Nevertheless, an individual of judgment can learn from others what to avoid and what to emulate, and therefore can shape and develop his own qualities for the better.

Even though there is a paucity of good memoirs and biographies, particularly in the lower echelons of command, this material is the best available for an understanding of character, of the characteristics of men, of good and bad leadership, and of the influence of eminent personalities upon events. Military works *dealing with the rank and file,* such as Bolton's *The Private Soldier Under Washington* and Wiley's *Billy Yank,* should be read with the realization that bad soldiers tend to leave many documents behind them, while good soldiers ordinarily leave only the briefest sort of records or merely a name. For this reason even so-called "factual studies" of the fighting men are usually heavily loaded on the seamy side of life.

If study of leadership is to be profitable, the student must analyze, evaluate, and judge the qualities of both fighting men and leaders, with due regard to the circumstances and conditions under which they worked. But as the British scholar, Wilkinson, has said, "This judgment must never degenerate into mere negative criticism. . . ."[13] It should enable the thoughtful individual to determine and identify in others the desirable traits of soldiers and leaders in both staff and command positions. This should enable a military man to become a practical psychologist and should thus enable him to avoid becoming a mere theorist. As Clausewitz has pointed out, a commander "need not be a close observer of men, a sharp dissector of human character, but he must know the character, the feelings, the habits, the peculiar faults and inclinations of those whom he is to command."[14]

To be of maximum value in teaching military leadership, historical works must be factual and frank. Propagandistic or censored history is dangerous and should not be used, for it can provide no sound lessons or basis of professional training. It leads to false conclusions and fosters one of the worst evils in professional military thinking—self-deception. Histories written during the lives of the actors or too near their era are generally tinged with prejudice, colored by self-interested flattery, and influenced by the selective treatment of source material. Histories written too long after the time of the participants are frequently fictional or sentimental. Therefore, history will never be entirely satisfactory for instruction in leadership until it gives a complete picture of the participants—their

[13] Spencer Wilkinson, *The Brain of the Army* (Westminster, 1895), pp. 164–67.
[14] Clausewitz, *op. cit.*, I, p. 116.

merits, faults, temperaments, and ambitions, their Janus faces, their ability to exercise self-control especially in adversity, and their physical and mental conditions.[15]

Although the study of great captains is important to all military men, the study of "followship," as exemplified by subordinate leaders and staff officers, is equally important and perhaps more so because few can rise to the topmost position and even these must pass through the various grades in both staff and command assignments. Gen. Malin Craig, former Chief of Staff of the U. S. Army, emphasized this aspect of a military career in this advice to a graduating class at the U. S. Military Academy:

> No young officer can be unconscious of the impression he is making on others. And yet he would be wrong to govern his conduct solely by the opinions of others. First of all he must to himself be true. Fortunately, by a happy paradox of human nature we best serve ourselves when we think only of serving others. An officer . . . should make it a cardinal principle of life that by no act of commission or omission on his part will he permit his immediate superior to make a mistake. Once an officer establishes such a professional reputation his future is assured. His services will be eagerly sought and his assignment to duties of the highest importance is certain.[16]

A comprehensive knowledge of military history emphasizing both leadership and followship will facilitate mutual respect and understanding in the armed forces; the broad problems of the higher commanders will be more readily comprehended by subordinates, and the complex human, material, and physical problems of the soldier and of the small-unit commanders better appreciated by superiors. Such understanding will greatly facilitate good morale in any organization.

Military History in Instruction and Training

Military history is the very foundation of our knowledge of tactics and strategy. It is also the foundation on which the theoretical and practical training of troops and the development of training directives are based. It gives life to the bare bones of facts and regulations. An instructor who is not grounded in military history appropriate to the level of his instruction is dry and pedantic and will accomplish no great results. On the other hand, one who not only knows the principles but who also can illustrate them with historical examples, giving facts concerning troops, commanders, weapons, supply, communications, terrain, and weather, can give life to his

---

[15] MS B-298 (Blumentritt), pp. 7–9. Applied Studies Br., OCMH. This study on the writing of military history was written in 1946 by General der Infanterie Guenther Blumentritt, formerly chief of staff of the German Commander in Chief West.

[16] Gen. Malin Craig, CofS of the U. S. Army, Address, at the Graduation Exercises, U. S. Military Academy, 12 June 1937.

instruction and make it useful.   This is just as true in troop training as in formal instruction in military schools.   Above all else, however, military history gives an interesting and deep insight into the minds and hearts of military men, into tactical and strategical methods, procedures, and principles, and into the relations between war, politics, economy, philosophy, geography, and the mentality of nations and races.[17]

If military history is to be of greatest value in instruction and training it must be more than a logical, factual record or account of events.   After the facts have been synthesized into an effective record there is a final step in the project—the analysis of the facts and the formulation of conclusions based on that analysis.   This last step can be taken only by one who is both well grounded in historiography and professionally qualified to deal with the military organization and the operations recorded.   In dealing with these subjects at the higher levels the analyst must have a knowledge of national policy, of the higher organization for war, of military geography, of strategy and grand tactics, of logistics and techniques of the combined arms, and of weapons.   At the lower levels of military organizations and operations the analyst must have a knowledge of troop psychology, of weapons, of terrain, of weather and climate, and of tactics, logistics, and techniques of the combined arms.

Military History and Planning

According to Gen. Charles L. Bolte, former Vice Chief of Staff, Department of the Army: "The past must be studied as the basis for, and a guide to, the study of the future.   To make a sound prediction one must project the past into the future.   If the past is ignored . . . there is no firm foundation for sound forecasting, sound planning, sound apportioning of the limited means . . . available or to become available." [18]   If the limited means of manpower, industrial capacity, and resources are squandered, even inadvertently, the nation will suffer accordingly—perhaps disastrously.

General Bolte further points out, "A close examination and study of the period immediately prior to and following the outbreak of a war" will prove of great value to all those responsible for long-range planning.   It is in these periods that the effect of past policies and plans or lack of plans becomes most evident, because errors quickly and decisively influence the course of events.   Such errors are particularly serious because they can be overcome, if at all, only at great expense and with the loss of precious time.

[17] MS B–298 (Blumentritt), *op. cit.*

[18] Maj Gen Charles L. Bolte, "The Role of Land Forces in Future Wars," *U. S. Naval Institute Proceedings*, Vol. 75 (January 1949), p. 26.

History shows conclusively that weapons have a decisive influence upon military operations. The development of weapons should therefore be of particular concern to planners, for it takes years to improve or make new weapons and to insure their proper integration into an organization.

Military History and Changes in Tactics and Techniques

One of the most important lessons a military student can learn from history is the necessity of quickly recognizing the changes in tactics and technique which are indicated during the course of a war, and especially during the meeting engagement. It is at these times that secret weapons and differences in tactics and techniques show up most clearly and require immediate adjustment to conditions on the battlefield. History teaches that commanders must react quickly to the new conditions and at the same time transmit information to higher commanders concerning the circumstances and occurrences on the battlefield which indicate a need for changes in equipment, tactics, and techniques.

The study of the initial phases of military operations deserves special attention. These are periods that mark the introduction of new weapons, new tactics, or inexperienced troops; that involve a sudden shift in type of terrain, in defensive arrangements, in weather, or in seasonal conditions. It is during these periods that faulty organization, inadequate or impractical training, inefficient weapons, failure of leadership and communications, inadequate logistical support, faulty coordination of the various arms, unforeseen effect of weather and terrain, rumors, and many other factors, some almost intangible, create a state of confusion which should challenge every military student. Knowledge gained through a study of the initial phases of past operations will pay untold dividends to those who may be involved later in similar situations.

Learning from Experience and Experiences of Others

A military student should not allow personal experience on the battlefield to limit his point of view but should add to it the experiences of others.[19] Conclusions and principles based on a single personal experience or an inadequate preparation in military history are very dangerous. Ardant du Picq, a profound student of combat, has expressed the matter in another way. In a questionnaire submitted to contemporaries he said "Whoever has seen, turns to a method based on his knowledge, his personal experience as a

---

[19] Friedrich von Bernhardi, *On War of Today* (London, 1912), pp. 44–46.

soldier. But experience is long and life is short. The experiences of each cannot therefore be completed except by those of others." [20] In short, a careful study of objective military history with an open mind and with the determination of learning from the experiences of others will be of great benefit to any military student.

The principles of strategy have been evolved from an analytical study of many wars. They are, therefore, based on a great many experiences of the past and are immutable. "Consequently," as Gen. Douglas MacArthur has said, "the Army extends its analytical interest to the dust-buried accounts of wars long past as well as to those still reeking with the scent of battle" [21] with the object of the search dictating the field for its pursuit.

In the field of tactics and techniques, doctrine based on personal experience or the experience of others is apt to lead to error, for, as General MacArthur has also said, "In every age these [tactics] are decisively influenced by the characteristics of weapons currently available and by the means at hand for maneuvering, supplying, and controlling combat forces." [22] Leadership, organization, communications, training, morale, terrain, weather and climatic conditions, and the enemy will also differ as well as many other things. Peacetime tactical doctrine, therefore, can be determined only by a process of reasoning, by studying experiences of others in the most recent wars, and by experimentation. When doctrine has been subjected to test in actual battle it should be quickly readjusted to conform to reality and kept in step with conditions during the entire course of operations.

Military History and Learning from the Vanquished

Upon the conclusion of a war the victors decide how they should organize and equip for the future. They base their conclusions on their own experiences, which, no matter how great, are limited. It might be said that the victors reorganize on the basis of considerable self-esteem, attributing their success to better organization, equipment, training and leadership, while the vanquished reorganize on the basis of considerable humility, analyzing events and determining and eliminating weaknesses with the intention of defeating the recent enemy. Military progress is therefore slow among the victors because conceit and complacency too often have the upper hand. The vanquished, however, looking further ahead, build new organization and new equipment. This lesson should be carefully heeded by the United States: having won all the wars in which it

[20] Ardant du Picq, *Battle Studies*, trans. John N. Greely (Harrisburg, 1947), p. 8.

[21] Gen Douglas MacArthur, *Annual Report of the Chief of Staff for the Fiscal Year ending June 30, 1935*, p. 72.

[22] *Ibid.*

has engaged it is in a certain degree of danger because history reveals that military victory has frequently contained the seeds of weakness, deficiencies in coordination, training, discipline, and leadership, inefficiencies in organization and logistical arrangements, inadequacies of intelligence, and shortcomings of equipment and supply.

The most convincing lessons can be learned from defeats. But it is infinitely better to learn from the defeats of others. It is, therefore, advantageous to study and analyze the records of the vanquished. The student of military history should give careful consideration to the writings of the leaders of defeated nations who have been allowed to express themselves unhampered by censorship. Frequently, much more can be learned from them than from the leaders of victorious nations who are apt to pass over the unfavorable matters and leave the impression that few mistakes were made. The veil of censorship usually continues in victorious nations where the proprieties are at least insisted upon and military regulations and discipline are at hand to enforce them.

Military History in Preparation for the Higher Direction of Military Affairs

The American Revolution was but the prelude to the era of peoples' wars, the wild and desperate struggles that have grown in intensity and destructiveness down to the present time. As Marshal Foch has said: " . . . they [the peoples] were to set themselves the goal, not a dynastic interest, not of the conquest or possession of a province, but the defence or the propagation of philosophical ideas in the first place, next of principles of independence, of unity, of immaterial advantages of various kinds. Lastly they staked upon the issue the interests and fortune of every individual private. Hence the rising of passions, that is elements of force, hitherto in the main unused." [23]

In the United States, the direction of the armed forces is vested in the civilian Chief of State or President and the policy matters in the Congress. The Executive and the Congress are elected to office and have not often been trained or soundly experienced in military affairs. The President must of necessity coordinate the vast executive agencies of the government in both peace and war. He must understand the various agencies, the contributions they can make to the national security, as well as their requirements. He must also be capable of convincing the policy-making body or Congress of the necessity for these requirements. At the same time he must be capable of decentralizing the execution of tasks to subordinates.

[23] Ferdinand Foch, *The Principles of War*, trans. Hillare Belloc (New York, 1920), p. 30.

13

As General Maurice has pointed out, much of the difficulty in the relations between statesman and soldier has arisen in the past because of a misconception of what is meant by the conduct of war.[24] Too many military men have thought of it as the direction of the armed forces in actual operations.   Today, however, it implies the direction of the entire power and resources of the nation in pursuit of national objectives and their coordination with those of allies. This is certainly not the responsibility of the highest ranking military commanders even though they are intimately concerned in them because of their bearing upon the preparation and organization of the nation for war.   On the civilian side the statesmen are generally even less prepared for their role in a national emergency because the civilian educational system in the United States has long neglected the study of war.   Those who have aspired to high government positions have had to prepare themselves on their own initiative and without satisfactory guidance.

The soundest preparation for an understanding of the delicate relationship of statesman and soldier and of their mutual problems in the conduct of military affairs in peace and war can be made by studying history—particularly American history of the periods preceding, during, and following national emergencies.   Unfortunately, future statesmen are rarely sure of their place in sufficient time to make the necessary preparation.   Personnel of the armed forces are in much better position to foresee their future roles in war than those unknown ones who will someday be their superiors.   They should, therefore, conscientiously prepare themselves for the supporting roles of advisers to the paramount civilian authorities and of instructors to the American people.   Both roles will require great moral courage if the public interests are to be best served.   An improperly prepared individual or a base flatterer may rise to the position of chief adviser on the basis of personality and lead his superiors and the country to ruin.   The bloody pages of history are replete with examples of this kind.

Today, every element of national strength—ideological, spiritual, psychological, political, financial, economic, technological, and military—is involved in war and in the preparation for war.   Even worse, imperialistic communism has made conflict a continuing and continuous activity among the people in every land in the world. The very name *war* has become too restrictive.   *Universal conflict* better describes the relations of man to man, of people to people, and of state to state in the shrunken world of the 20th century.

Now, less than ever before, can responsible military leaders ignore the broad fields of knowledge involved in this concept of *universal conflict*.   Accordingly, military leaders who are responsible for advice

---

[24] Frederick Maurice, *Governments and War* (London, 1926), pp. 118–28.

on strategy should be versed in the broader aspects of all of these matters and should bring to their task a balanced judgment capable of giving to each the correct value it deserves in solving problems that arise in a rapidly changing world.

Above everything else, however, American military leaders should have a knowledge of their own land and its people and of its military history. Without this fundamental knowledge decisions might sooner or later transcend the practical and realistic. This could result in a national catastrophe.

Military History in the Education of the American People

After long and distinguished service, Lt. Gen. John M. Schofield concluded that general military education is essential in a country having a popular government. "No man [he wrote] can be fully qualified for the duties of statesman until he has made a thorough study of the science of war in its broadest sense. . . . [Otherwise] he is liable to do almost infinite damage to his country." [25] Although this lesson was pointed out even earlier and the Morrill Act of 1862 was designed to improve the situation, military education is still woefully neglected in American educational institutions and the people give little consideration to the military qualifications of those who seek their support for important positions in the government.

Thus it can be seen that military students can render an important service to the people of the United States and to government officials by clarifying the causes and characteristics of war, the principles underlying the conduct of alliances, the coordination of domestic, foreign, and military policy, and the conditions governing the conduct of operations and the men who fight them.

As Burchardt has pointed out, the history of our country should be considered in parallel with that of other nations and in relation to world history and its laws—a part of a greater whole. [26] This will require not only an understanding of the histories of existing nations but of those, once powerful, but now gone forever.

The role of instructor to the people is, however, a difficult and unprofitable one. Many of those who have attempted the role have lacked objectivity and, in their zeal, adopted propagandistic techniques. Even the best have been accused of war mongering by opponents who themselves were nurturing the seeds of war.

---

[25] John M. Schofield, *Forty-six Years in the Army* (New York, 1897), p. 516.
[26] Jacob Burchardt, *Force and Freedom* (New York, 1943), pp. 89–90.

CHAPTER II
THE STUDY OF AMERICAN MILITARY HISTORY

General

The study of history is one which can be carried on without a teacher and even without access to a large library. This is indeed fortunate, for officers of the military services are of necessity widely scattered and subject to frequent changes of station. Besides, no profession can benefit more directly from the study of history than the military, for as Marshal Foch has said, ". . . no study is possible on the battlefield; one does there simply what *one can* in order to apply what *one* knows."[1] But study time available to an officer is limited and becomes even more limited during periods of national emergency and when increased rank means added responsibility. At a time when one emergency blends into another, it is, therefore, more important than ever that an officer should avoid wasting unrecoverable time on historical material of questionable value. One of the simplest ways to do this is to avoid books of doubtful value and to have a planned reading program.

Military books, like others, vary in quality, each reflecting the character of the author and the purpose he had in view. Some writers may take a historical subject, but write a piece of fiction. Unthinking readers praise the book as interesting, forgetting that history is a science and not literature. Some books are written to deceive. Some few, however, show an author with a judicious temperament who spares no pains to search for evidence and, when found, weighs it carefully and intelligently. These are the best authors, who must be found by the historian and student of history, if precious time is to be conserved and history is to be advantageously used by the Army.

A general idea of the scope and quality of a military history or biography may be obtained by reading the book reviews published coincident with the release of the work by the publisher. Reviews of this type, particularly those in newspapers, and, to a less extent, in the commercial magazines, are not always careful or objective. Reviews in such media are sometimes influenced by the author, publisher, or editorial policy of the newspaper or magazine concerned. Many papers concoct their reviews from publishers' adver-

---

[1] Foch, *op. cit.*

tisements and notices. Reviews of historical works in learned journals are infinitely preferrable to newspaper reviews, for such journals generally use the services of recognized experts in their fields. But the final judgment on the value of a military work is the responsibility of the student or historian, who should develop a system of examining such works. A system has been suggested by one of the Army's eminent historians, Col. Oliver L. Spaulding.[2] Somewhat modified it is as follows:

The first clue to the value of a book is found on the title page. The title page often gives an indication of the author's official or professional standing, such as military rank or academic connections and degrees, etc. It is also of value to know under whose auspices the book was written. When this information is not contained on the title page, it is usually found in the preface. The author may be a most distinguished person along certain lines, but it does not follow that all books by authors who appear to lack professional qualifications should be rejected. They may prove very useful when properly evaluated. Sometimes the very best of books have been written by men whose qualifications, as given on the title page, do not appear adequate. ·

A second clue to the value of a book is found in the preface. This should be read carefully. It should tell why and how the book was written and furnish an indication of the writer's point of view. It frequently tells from whom the author has had advice and assistance in the preparation of the book. It may give a review of the material used and should tell whether the writer is presenting any newly discovered evidence or a new point of view, if it is a new book on a subject already thoroughly covered.

A third clue to the value of the book is the bibliographical note or bibliography and the nature and extent of the documentation. The reader should determine whether the book is a mere reinterpretation of events based on secondary sources, or an original contribution based upon new or heretofore unused sources. Even a new presentation of old material, however, need not necessarily damn the book. A great number of works have been produced on a certain subject over a period of years. Sometimes there is a positive need for a new and better presented book on the same subject.

A fourth clue which gives information concerning the specific value of a book for a certain purpose is found in the table of contents, printed at the beginning of a book, and in the index, printed at the rear. These parts of a work will furnish a clue as to whether

---

[2] Lecture, Col Oliver L. Spaulding, "Books, How to Judge Them and How to Use Them," before the Army War College, 2 Oct 22. Reprinted by OCMH, DA, July 1953.

or not the book covers the prescribed subjects desired. A military history or biography which lacks a comprehensive index covering the broad range of all military activities, although otherwise of high value, may be of limited value, because it lacks the key which would make its contents readily available.

A systematic use of book reviews and of the four clues described above will lead to the discard of many books and will direct the student's attention to the particular parts of those he wishes to study.

The military knowledge which Marshal Foch believed necessary cannot be acquired entirely at the service schools and colleges. Much of it must be obtained through the initiative and personal effort of the officer himself and on his own time.

Any satisfactory program for self-improvement should be progressive and appropriate to the grade of the student. The works included should provide the officer with professional background *appropriate to his level of responsibility* and eventually with an ever-broadening understanding of military art and science and of the relationship of military policy to the foreign and economic policies of the United States. Thus it is that the program should help develop an officer corps possessing the wisdom essential to the successful performance of duties in the higher staff and command positions. In the past this progressive aspect of historical study has been neglected with the result that officers have tended to prepare themselves for the role of war lord, such as Alexander, Frederick the Great, or Napoleon, or a great military leader such as Hannibal, Scipio, Caesar, Marlborough, Washington, Grant, Lee, or Foch, instead of preparing for their more probable assignments or fields of responsibility and the ones next above. As a result, too many American military men have neglected the basic aspects of their professional preparation.

According to the best authorities man and his reactions to combat have changed less than other elements in war. Regardless of improvements in materiel man still reacts very much as he has always reacted in battle. And he probably will always react in about the same way. It is for this reason that the closest attention must be given to the fighting man and to the basic problem of leadership. These two subjects constitute the foundation upon which all other knowledge of the military art and science should be based. Accordingly, the study of these subjects should begin early in an officer's career and continue, in ever-expanding fashion, throughout his service.

The study of military history should also be solidly based on the problems of the squad, platoon, company, battalion, combat team or command, and division. Here, where results of decisions and actions are most immediate, wisdom and a knowledge of American military operations gleaned from the study of history can be used most advantageously. Unfortunately, material dealing with these problems is rather limited. Although some progress has been made to fill the void much work remains to be done in the field of small-unit history.

Students of the past should also consider events in light of the times and conditions under review. The geography, communications, population, education and culture, military forces and armament, resources, industry and manufactures, scientific development, and political, religious, economic, medical, and sociological conditions of the period must be understood before events can be properly evaluated and lessons derived therefrom. Quite obviously this is a difficult task.

Finally, the military student should be familiar with the works of the military philosophers because they have had a profound influence upon military thinking and literature and, therefore, upon the operational manuals or field service regulations of nearly all nations. The great military thinkers have not belonged to any one race or time. They have all been profound students of history and many of them have also had personal experience in war. Sun Tzu in *The Art of War,* Vegetius in *The Military Institutions of the Romans,* Clausewitz in *On War,* Jomini in *The Art of War,* DuPicq in *Battle Studies,* Von Schlieffen in *Cannae,* Mahan in *Influence of Sea Power on History,* Foch in *Principles of War,* Douhet in *The Command of the Air,* Fuller in *Foundation of the Science of War,* DeGaulle in *The Army of the Future,* Kingston-McCloughry in *War in Three Dimensions,* and others have used history to distill strategical and tactical principles which affect the conduct of war. Other scholars such as Machiavelli in the *Prince and the Discourses,* Grotius in *The Law of War and Peace,* DeVattel in *The Law of Nations,* Lea in *Valor of Ignorance,* Fairgrieve in *Geography and World Power,* Mackinder in *Democratic Ideals and Reality,* and Simonds and Emeny in *Great Powers and World Politics,* have treated some of the over-riding factors, such as political, economic, and geographical, which concern the conduct of war.

A careful study of such works should enable the military student *who has mastered the basic subjects of his profession* to comprehend the lessons that are to be learned from history. The wisdom acquired by reading and studying the experiences of others should enable him to recognize in any given situation the time and place for the application of principles to the solution of current problems and thus avoid the misinterpretation or overemphasis of certain principles which has proved so catastrophic to other nations in the past.

The progressive reading list which follows is adjusted to length of service and therefore to grade and to the Army school system. Any military student can use the list to advantage even if he is never admitted to the higher military colleges. But no military student can acquire the maximum benefit from the Army schools and colleges without systematic historical study because military history is the foundation upon which instruction in leadership and in strategical, tactical, and logistical matters is based.

Few individuals will be able to study all the books listed. Each should, however, examine the books and select the ones that have special appeal. Other works should also be added according to the tastes, interests, and assignment of the individual because the list does not include all that a military student should study. Each arm and service and each special assignment will require additional reading and study. Besides there are broader fields of culture and science with which forward-looking officers must keep abreast. In this connection it is well to consider the words of Mahan and the admonition given by him in a less hectic period of our history:

> . . . master and keep track of the great current events in history contemporary with yourself, appreciate their meaning. Your own profession, on its military side, calls of course for your first and closest attention; but you all will have time enough to read military history, appreciating its teachings, and you can also keep abreast of international relations to such an extent that when you reach positions of prime responsibility, your glance—your *coup d'oeil*, to repeat the French idiom—will quickly take in the whole picture of your country's interests in every emergency, whether that be pressing or remote . . . aim to be yourselves statesmen as well as seamen. . . .[3]

In reality, the books included here are but the basic works with which all well-informed American officers should be familiar. If the books are not available in post, camp, or station libraries, they probably can be secured on an inter-library loan from one of the larger libraries generally found at the service schools or colleges or from the Army Library, Pentagon, Washington 25, D. C.

Finally, as a word of caution, it is well to consider the views of General Schofield. He has observed that study or scholarship alone cannot fully qualify a man for a responsible role in war, either "as commanders in the field, for which no amount of theoretical education alone can qualify a man, . . . or as military advisers." [4] For such important assignments nothing can take the place of *practical experience.*

[3] Alfred T. Mahan, *Naval Strategy* (Boston, 1919), pp. 20–21.
[4] Schofield, *op. cit.*, p. 516.

A Progressive Course of Study in American Military History [5]

Historical Reading in First Five Years' Service

General

The Constitution of the United States of America and *The Declaration of Independence*	
American Military History: 1607–1953	ROTCM 145–20
History of the United States Navy	Knox
Decisive Battles of the United States	Fuller
The American Republic	Beard
Roots of Strategy	Phillips
War Through the Ages	Montross
The Foundation of the Science of War	Fuller
Armament and History	Fuller
The Military Staff	Hittle
The History of Sea Power	Stevens and Westcott

The Fighting Man [6]

Battle Studies	DuPicq
The Private Soldier Under Washington	Bolton
The Life of Johnny Reb	Wiley
The Life of Billy Yank	Wiley
A Rifleman Went to War	McBride
Men Against Fire	Marshall
The Medal of Honor of the United States Army	Department of the Army

Leadership [7]

Psychology for the Armed Services	Boring
Leadership, FM 22–10	Department of the Army
Preparation for Leadership in America	Robinett (ed.)
Autobiography	Franklin
Montcalm and Wolfe	Parkmann

---

[5] The course of study includes a number of basic works written by foreign authors. These works are included because of the important influence they have had or should have upon American military thinking.

[6] In studying secondary military works dealing with the fighting men, the student should realize that bad soldiers generally leave many personal records behind them while good soldiers leave few. Most writers who tried to show the fighting men as they actually were have unconsciously overemphasized the activities of the bad soldiers by drawing heavily upon reports of investigations and records of courts-martial.

[7] A student of military leadership pressed for time may find it advantageous to refer to short biographical sketches found in the *Dictionary of American Biography*.

390016 O – 56 – 3

Leadership—Continued

General von Steuben........................	Palmer
Memoirs of the War in the Southern Department of the United States........................	Lee
Light-Horse Harry Lee........................	Boyd
Anthony Wayne........................	Wildes
"First with the Most" Forrest........................	Henry
Glory Hunter: A Life of General Custer...........	Van De Water
War Years with Jeb Stuart........................	Blackford
Ranger Mosby........................	Jones
Fix Bayonets!........................	Thomason
Company Commander........................	MacDonald

Operations

Appeal to Arms—A Military History of the American Revolution........................	Wallace
Indian Fighting Army........................	Downey
The Defence of Duffer's Drift (Fiction)...........	Swinton
Infantry in Battle........................	Infantry School
Small Unit Actions in Korea........................	Gugeler
Small Unit Actions during the German Campaign in Russia........................	DA Pamphlet 20–269
Three Battles: Arnaville, Altuzzo and Schmidt........	
Combat Support in Korea........................	

Historical Reading—Five to Ten Years' Service

General

The Art of War........................	Sun Tzu
Cannae........................	Von Schlieffen
On War........................	Clausewitz
The Principles of War........................	Foch
Machine Warfare........................	Fuller
The Army of the Future........................	DeGaulle

Leadership

Power of Personality in War........................	Freytag-Loringhoven
Life of Major General Nathanael Greene...........	Greene
Tarnished Warrior, Major General James Wilkinson..	Jacobs
Oliver Hazard Perry........................	Dutton
Captain Sam Grant........................	Lewis
Stonewall Jackson and the Civil War...........	Henderson
Lee's Lieutenants—A Study in Command........	Freeman
Personal Memoirs of Gen. W. T. Sherman........	Sherman
Sherman—Fighting Prophet........................	Lewis
Jeb Stuart........................	Thomason

Leadership—Continued

Operations

Historical Reading—Ten to Fifteen Years' Service

General

Leadership

Leadership—Continued

Admiral Farragut	Mahan
A Soldier's Story	Bradley
Admiral Halsey's Story	Halsey
General Kenney Reports	Kenney

Operations

History of the Civil War, 1861–65	Rhodes
Lessons of Allied Co-operation: Naval, Military and Air 1914–1918	Maurice
Operations in Northwest Africa, 1942–43	Howe
Europe: Torch to Pointblank	Craven and Cate
Operations in North African Waters October 1942–June 1943	Morison
Naval Lessons of the Great War	Kittredge
Okinawa: The Last Battle	Appleman, Burns, Gugeler, and Stevens

Historical Reading—Fifteen to Twenty-five Years' Service

General

The Peloponnesian War	Thucydides
The Prince and the Discourses	Machiavelli
The Rise of Rail-Power in War and Conquest, 1833–1914	Pratt
Force and Freedom: Reflections on History	Burchardt
The Impact of War	Herring
Valor of Ignorance	Lea
War in Three Dimensions	Kingston-McCloughry
Governments and War	Maurice
The Crowd, A Study of the Popular Mind	Le Bon
A Diplomatic History of the United States	Bemis
American Democracy and Military Power	Smith
The President, Office and Powers	Corwin
The Presidents and Civil Disorder	Rich
American Industry in War	Baruch
Propaganda for War, the Campaign Against American Neutrality, 1914–1917	Peterson
Spreading the Germs of Hate	Viereck
How We Advertised America	Creel
America's Munitions, 1917–1918	Crowell
Mobilization Planning and the National Security	Elliott
The Strange Alliance	Deane
The Purse and the Sword, 1933–1950	Huzar
Lend-Lease Weapon for Victory	Stettinius
Arsenal of Democracy	Nelson

General— Continued

Scientists Against Time . . . . Baxter
The Supreme Command . . . . Pogue
Stilwell's Mission to China . . . . Romanus and
                                                 Sunderland
Strategic Planning for Coalition Warfare . . . . Snell and Matloff
DA Pam 20–212, *History of Military Mobilization in* Kreidberg and
   the United States Army, 1775–1945 . . . . Henry
DA Pam 20–211, *The Personnel Replacement System*
   in the United States Army . . . . Lerwill
DA Pam 20–210, *History of Personnel Demobilization*
   in the United States Army . . . . Sparrow

Leadership

George Washington . . . . Freeman
Washington, Commander-in-Chief . . . . Frothingham
John C. Calhoun . . . . Wiltse
James K. Polk . . . . McCormac
Lincoln Finds a General . . . . Williams
Personal Memoirs of U. S. Grant . . . . Grant
Forty-Six Years in the Army . . . . Schofield
Woodrow Wilson and the World War . . . . Seymour
Newton D. Baker, America at War . . . . Palmer
The Nation at War . . . . March
My Experiences in the World War . . . . Pershing
Washington, Lincoln, Wilson: Three War Statesmen . . . Palmer
Roosevelt and Hopkins: An Intimate History . . . . Sherwood
On Active Service in Peace and War . . . . Stimson and
                                                 Bundy
I Was There . . . . Leahy
Fleet Admiral King: A Naval Record . . . . King and Muir
Global Mission . . . . Arnold
Crusade in Europe . . . . Eisenhower

Operations

Chief of Staff: Prewar Plans and Preparations . . . . Watson
The Washington Command Post . . . . Cline
The Battle of the Atlantic, September 1939–May 1943 . . Morison
Cross-Channel Attack . . . . Harrison
Break Out and Pursuit . . . . Blumenson
The Lorraine Campaign . . . . Cole
Europe: ARGUMENT to V E Day . . . . Craven and Cate
Persian Corridor and Aid to Russia . . . . Motter
Great Mistakes of the War . . . . Baldwin

CHAPTER III
SOURCES OF INFORMATION

General

This chapter explains the sources from which information bearing upon American military operations or activities may be obtained. Anyone who aspires to write serious American military history must be familiar with the sources and must become expert in using them. This preparation should be made before undertaking any historical writing. There is a tendency for inexperienced students to attempt this preparation incidental to research but this is a bad mistake and should be avoided.

The following works may serve as aids to a military historian:

Allen, F. Sturges. *Allen's Synonyms and Antonyms.* Edited by T. H. Vail Motter. New York, 1938.

Aston, Sir George (ed.). *A Study of War.* London, 1927.

Channing, Edward, Albert Bushnel Hart, Frederick J. Turner. *Guide to the Study and Writing of American History,* Boston, 1912.

Flynn, Fred M. *The Writing of History, an Introduction to Historical Method.* New Haven, 1920.

Fortescue, J. W. *Military History.* Cambridge, 1914.

Fowler, H. W. *Dictionary of Modern English Usage.* London, 1926.

Hart, B. H. Liddell. *Why Don't We Learn from History?* London, 1944.

Hockett, Homer Carey. *Introduction to Research in American History.* 2d ed.; New York, 1949.

Johnson, Allen. *The Historian and Historical Evidence.* New York, 1926.

Langer, William L. *An Encyclopedia of World History.* Boston, 1948.

Langlois, Charles V. and Charles Seignobos. *Introduction to the Study of History.* Translated by G. Berry. New York, 1912.

Oman, Charles. *On the Writing of History.* London, 1914.

Parker, Donald D. *Local History.* New York, 1944.

Perrin, G. Porter. *Writer's Guide and Index to English.* New York, 1944.

Scott, A. P. and J. L. Cate. *Syllabus and Problems for History 201, Introduction in Historical Method and Historiography.* Chicago, 1945.

United States Army—Memo W345–21–43, 3 Aug 43, "Military History of the Second World War."   SR 320–5–1, Aug 50, "Dictionary of United States Army Terms."

United States Government Printing Office Style Manual.   Washington, 1953.   [*See also* Appendix A.]

Webster's New International Dictionary.   2d rev. ed.; Springfield, 1954.   [According to the GPO *Style Manual* "Webster's New International Dictionary . . . has been the accepted authority for Government printing for more than 85 years . . . [and GPO] will continue to follow Webster's spelling."]

Personnel Having Knowledge of Military Events

Most history is written from documents long after the conclusion of the events recorded.   But the historian frequently has direct access to eyewitnesses or participants in military events and, whenever possible, he should avail himself of their knowledge.   This enables a historian to gain a better understanding of events, check statements in the records, to determine the varying points of view in case of disputes, and to improve the vividness and precision of his narrative.   He does this by conducting interviews or by submitting questionnaires to those who appear to have the information needed.   In either case the historian can obtain the best results only by making a thorough preparation in advance.

After studying all available written materials, the historian should know if there are any gaps in the story.   He can then make a plan for the interview or interrogation of individuals who may have the information needed to complete his project.   The historian must know as precisely as possible what kind of information he needs and must have a solid grasp of the problem or of the events under study. If the events are still in progress, the success of the project will depend greatly upon the thoroughness and promptness of the preparation and of the interview.   If a questionnaire is to be used some time after the conclusion of events under study, the preparation can be much more deliberate.

The knowledge, personality, and skill of the historian will determine to a considerable degree his success in an interview.   By guarding against generalizations, prejudice, lack of objectivity, bias, secondhand evidence, and other pitfalls, the historian may arrive at a true account of events.   For the most favorable results, he should combine the best traits and capabilities of historian, trial lawyer, and reporter.

The historian should record the results of an interview as soon as possible after it is completed.   If possible, the person interviewed should have an opportunity to correct the record.

Libraries and Archives: How to Use Them

Libraries: General Information

Researchers and Libraries

Upon initial contact with a library a researcher should make his identity and purpose known to the authorities concerned. At the same time he should inquire about the rules and regulations of the institution—and be ready to abide by them. Librarians can attest to the need for this caution.

Next, he should familiarize himself with the operational methods of each establishment visited. In view of the fact that library procedures vary from place to place, such preliminary preparation may save much time. Some of the more important variations are summarized below in "Library Procedures."

Finally, the researcher should early ascertain the extent of the resources and facilities available in the library in which he plans to work. Some libraries issue a brochure, sometimes only a typewritten sheet, to inform readers on the general scope and arrangement of their collections.

Libraries and Research Work

Webster describes a library as: ". . . a building devoted to a collection of books, manuscripts, etc., kept for use but not for sale . . . an institution for the custody, circulation, or administration of such a collection. . . ."

Despite a multiplicity of designations, there are but three types of libraries: general libraries, covering practically the entire range of human knowledge and suitable for either serious work or for entertainment; research libraries, dedicated to one or more, usually closely correlated, fields of investigation; and special libraries, which are generally established for the benefit of particular groups.

Regardless of title or type, the value of any library to the researcher rests solely upon the nature and importance of its holdings and on the degree of accessibility to the information which they contain. To students of military history, libraries are primarily depositories of historical source and reference materials.

Obviously, researchers cannot always have access to a major library, such as the Library of Congress, where the facilities and resources are so great that it is internationally famous. This is no longer as important as it once was because the small institutions may contain unique materials, and modern developments, such as interlibrary loans and the microfilming of books or documents, have increased the usefulness of "local" libraries.

Reference to publications like the *Special Libraries Directory,* issued by the Special Libraries Association in 1935, or to the *American Library Directory—1951,* published by the R. R. Bowker Co. of New York, will provide detailed information concerning American and Canadian libraries.

Library Procedures

The Library Shelf

The terms "open and closed shelf" are frequently used by librarians and merit some explanation. From the researcher's standpoint, for example, it makes a great deal of difference whether or not he is granted "shelf privileges."

To librarians "shelving" means: the placing of books on library shelves in proper order. In other words, the library shelf is the "heart" of the institution, because it represents actual resources, properly arranged in suitable equipment and duly recorded. Consequently, from a technical point of view a "shelf list" is a record of books, arranged in the order in which they stand on the shelves.

In line with this same terminology, "open shelves" are those library shelves to which readers have direct access for the examination of books, while, conversely, "closed shelves" are those which are not available to the public or which, as in a university or in a private library, are open to a limited group only. It should be noted that the terms "shelf" and "stack" are synonymous expressions.

"Stack privileges" indicates that the holder thereof, usually identified by means of a "stack card," has been granted permission to examine books on certain shelves or stacks that are, therefore, "open" to him and that may be "closed" to others. This is a very valuable privilege, because it enables the researcher to make a rapid survey of materials on library shelves without going through the normal time-consuming routine.

Library Catalogues

According to the American Library Association's *Glossary of Library Terms* (Chicago, 1943), a library catalogue is: "A list of books, maps, etc., arranged according to some definite plan. As distinguished from a bibliography it is a list which records, describes, and indexes the resources of a collection, a library, or a group of libraries. . . ." Such a list may be in card form, with each entry on a separate card, or it may be in book form, wherein entries follow each other in some sort of sequence. More specifically, as well as normally, a card catalogue is one in which entries on separate cards are arranged in a definite order in library card trays or drawers.

Most of the American libraries now employ such card catalogues. Many of them have also adopted the so-called "dictionary catalogue" system wherein card entries (whether by author, title, or subject) and related references are arranged together under a single alphabet.

Various schemes are used in connection with library cataloguing processes to insure that materials described in the catalogues, whether in card or book form, can be readily identified or located—a procedure known as classification.

Classification Systems

There are many types of classification, but only book classification need be considered in this pamphlet. Briefly, classification is a scheme for arranging books and other material according to subject and form. Its purpose is to facilitate the use of reading materials; its function is to group similar things together.

Comparative Outline for Main (Subject) Classes or Schedules

Dewey Decimal (1876)	Cutter Expansive (1891)	Library of Congress (1899)
000 General Works	A References, General Works	A General Works
100 Philosophy	B–D Philosophy, Religion	B Philosophy, Religion
200 Religion		C–F History, Auxiliary Sciences
300 Sociology	E–G Historical Sciences, Biography, History, Geography, Travel	
400 Philology		G Geography
500 Pure Science		H–K Social, Political Sciences
600 Useful Arts		
700 Fine Arts		L Education
800 Literature	H–K Social, Political Sciences	M–N Fine Arts
900 History, including Geography, Biography	L Physical Science	P Language, Literature
	M–P Natural Sciences	Q Science
	Q–V Useful Arts	R Medicine
	W Fine Arts	S Agriculture
	X Philology	T Technology
	Y Literature	U Military Science
	Z Bibliography, Library Sciences	V Naval Science
		Z Bibliography, Library Science

Before entering upon his work in any library, a researcher should familiarize himself with the classification system in use. This will permit him to compare the book title with the assigned classification number on the catalogue card and to assure himself at a glance that title and subject are not at variance and that the book in question is or is not pertinent to his study. Of far more importance perhaps, especially where the researcher has been granted "stack privileges," such knowledge also enables him to locate books on the library

shelves with minimum loss of time.   Some libraries publish classification charts or post copies of such charts in conspicuous places for
the guidance of readers.   A classification chart is a synopsis of the
classification scheme adopted by the library concerned, and is designed to assist researchers and others in finding the books they desire.

Library procedures may vary from one library to another and
sometimes even within the departments of the same library.   For
example, in Washington the Library of Congress adheres to the classification scheme that bears its name; on the other hand, the Public
Library uses both the Dewey Decimal and the Cutter Expansive
systems.   Book classification schemes most in use in this country are
outlined above.

Dewey Decimal Classification

First published by Melvil Dewey in 1876 and enlarged many times
since, this system is used by many libraries in the United States, as
well as abroad.   It was the first American classification to achieve
international recognition; furthermore, since 1930 Dewey decimal
notations have been printed on many of the Library of Congress
catalogue cards.

The principles of this system are summarized in a series of tables
which form part of the basic manual.[1]   The scheme divides all
human knowledge into 10 main classes, represented by arabic numerals, and expressed by three-digit figures, as 000, 100, 200, and
so forth; the "zero" (000) class being reserved for general publications such as periodicals and dictionaries, which cannot be definitely
assigned to any one of the other nine classes.   Each of these main
classes in turn is divided into 10 subclasses, with further decimal
subdivisions within each subclass as needed.   Additional subdivisions
can be provided by using a decimal point and placing supplementary numbers to the right of the decimal point.   For example:

A main class —	900	HISTORY
Subclasses —	910	Geography and travels
	920	Biography
	970	North America
	973	United States
	973.1	discovery –1607
	973.9	20th century 1901–
	973.91	early 20th century 1901–
		World War I and II, 1917–1921; 1939–

---

[1] Melvil Dewey, *Decimal Classification and Relative Index* (14th ed., rev. and enl.; Lake
Placid, N. Y., 1942).

Successive revisions of the original scheme have resulted in the incorporation of numerous refinements, such as the assignment of specific blocks of numbers to philological and to geographical subjects. Moreover, although initially designed for classification by subject matter, a special table of "form" numbers, common to all classes and to many divisions, has been provided to facilitate further breakdown by written form. The use of these numbers, called "form distinctions," is illustrated below:

.1 Philosophies, theories, etc.
.2 Compends, outlines
.3 Dictionaries, cyclopedias
.4 Essays, lectures, letters, etc.
.5 Periodicals, magazines, etc.
.6 Societies, associations, transactions, reports, etc.
.7 Education, study, teaching, etc.
.8 Polygraphy, collections, etc.
.9 History

Two examples are as follows:

A main class — 300   SOCIAL SCIENCES

Subclasses — { 355   Military science
355.07   Military schools
      (*Note:* When subject number does not end in 0, a zero is prefixed to the form number.)

A main class — 600   USEFUL ARTS

Subclasses — { 620   Engineering
620.3   Dictionary of engineering terms

The numerical notations of the decimal classification are sometimes combined with letter symbols, a modification most frequently encountered in the field of literature, wherein alphabetical arrangement of books by author has become common library practice.

War Department (Department of the Army) Decimal System

This system, an adaptation of the Dewey decimal classification to military subjects, uses a mixed notation of letters and arabic numerals. It is fully described in *War Department Decimal File System,* a publication of The Adjutant General's Office which is compiled from data furnished by various War Department agencies. First issued in 1914, it was reprinted in June 1915 and in July 1917, and an abridgment appeared in September 1917 in connection with World War I. This was followed by a complete and revised edition in May 1918. The last revised edition was released in 1943.

This system is important to military students since it is the prescribed method of classification for all Army correspondence and a knowledge of its subject headings and symbol designations will facilitate identification of, and requests for, military records. However, this system extends back only to 1914 and before that date many War Department agencies had evolved individual classification schemes.

To cover subjects that arise subsequent to the release of the most recent *War Department Decimal File System,* the Office of The Adjutant General compiles a supplement for its own use and for possible inclusion in future editions of the manual.

Universal Decimal Classification (Classification Decimale Universelle)

This system, mentioned here because it is widely used by major European libraries, is an expansion of the Dewey decimal classification. It was evolved by a group of international bibliographers, who first met in 1895 in Brussels, and is known as the "Brussels Classification."

Under the guidance of the International Institute of Documentation, this classification system has been revised several times. The first edition, in French, appeared 1899–1905; a second French edition, in four volumes, was published 1927–1933; a German edition was begun in 1934; and a so-called fourth edition, in English, was issued in 1936.

Cutter (Expansive) Classification

This system, evolved by Charles A. Cutter, began to appear in print in 1891. It comprises seven separate, progressively more detailed, classification schedules; the seventh and last having been completed, insofar as possible, after the author's death, and published in 1904. Each of these schedules is intended to serve libraries of a given capacity, the complexity of the classification scheme increasing with the size of the library. This evolutionary feature gives the system its present designation: Expansive Classification.

Basically, it arranges all books into 26 classes, each of which is again divided into 26 parts, with further subdivision into still smaller groups; hence it is capable of almost unlimited expansion. Main classes are represented by large capitals, and subdivisions are represented by small capitals that are added to the letter which indicates main classes. These primary alphabetical notations have been supplemented by two tables of special numerical symbols; the first for form divisions, and the second, known as the "local list" (printed separately) for arrangement of materials according to geographical relation. Indexes are provided to facilitate the use of the system. There is one index for the first six classifications and a separate index for each of the completed parts of the seventh, or most detailed, classification.

The author of the Expansive Classification also devised two alphabetical order schemes which are extensively used by American libraries. These schemes, called "author-tables," consist of series of decimal numbers which are systematically combined with the initial letter or letters of surnames or words. One scheme uses two figures, the other three, and they are known as Cutter "Two-Figure" and "Three-Figure" tables, respectively. The "Cutter-Sanborn Three-Figure Table," a modern alteration of the Cutter "Two-Figure" author-table, is also in wide use.

Library of Congress Classification

This system, which dates from 1899, was developed by the Library of Congress to meet its own special requirements and while it includes features of several earlier schemes it follows the Cutter Classification most closely.

Because of its complexity, this system can best be understood by studying the official *Outline of the Library of Congress Classification,* issued by the Subject Catalogue Division. This edition was published in Washington in 1942 and reprinted in 1947. Subjects are broken down in 21 main classes, represented by letters of the alphabet. The letters, *I, O, W, X,* and *Y,* which have not yet been used, are available for possible future classes. Subdivisions of the main classes are indicated by designated series of arabic numerals, arranged consecutively within each group which can be further expanded by the addition of decimal notations; intentional gaps are provided within such sequences of numbers to permit insertion of new entries. In addition to the *Outline* mentioned above, Library of Congress schedules have been issued in pamphlet form, each main class being printed separately.

To illustrate the minute breakdown of subjects which is characteristic of this system of classification, extracts of the *Outline* pertaining to American military history are listed below:

C   History—Auxiliary Sciences
CB History of Civilization (General)
　　　Special countries in DA–DU, E, F
D   History and Topography (except America)
　　　　501–725 European War (World War I)
　　　　731–838 Second World War (World War II)

E   America (General) and United States (General)
   11–143 America (General)
   31– 45 North America (General)
   51– 99 Indians of North America
   101–135 Discovery of America
   151–810 United States
   151–185 General history and description
    185 Negroes in the United States
   186–199 Colonial Period
   201–298 Revolution
   351–364 War of 1812
   401–415 War with Mexico
   441–453 Slavery
   458–655 Civil War
   482–489 Confederate States
   714–735 War with Spain
    European war (1914–1918).   See D 501–680
    World War (1939–).   See D 731—
F   United States (Local) and America except the United States

Military Science

 U   Military science (General)
 UA Armies.   Organization and distribution
 UB Administration
 UC Maintenance and transportation
 UD Infantry
 UE Cavalry
 UF Artillery
 UG Military engineering
 UH Other services
   201–655 Medical and sanitary service

Naval Science

 V   Naval science (General)
 VA Navies.   Organization and distribution
 VB Naval administration
 VC Naval maintenance
 VD Naval seamen
 VE Marines
 VF Naval ordnance
 VG Other services of navies
   101–475 Medical and sanitary service

Library of Congress catalogue cards are used by a large number of other libraries, American and foreign. Following is a reproduction of a sample card.

MacDonald, Charles Brown, 1922–

Three battles: Arnaville, Altuzzo, and Schmidt, by Charles B. MacDonald and Sidney T. Mathews. Washington, Office of the Chief of Military History, Dept. of the Army, 1952.

xxiii, 443 p. illus. (part col.) maps (part col.) (United States Army in World War II: Special studies)

Part of illustrative matter inserted at end.
Includes bibliographical references.

1. Arnaville, Battle of, 1944. 2. Altuzzo, Battle of, 1944. 3. Schmidt, Battle of, 1944. I. Mathews, Sidney T. II. Title. (Series: U. S. Dept. of the Army. Office of Military History. United States Army in World War II)

D769.A533 vol. 8   pt. 1   940.542   52–61926

Library of Congress   [25]

Archival Collections

Researchers and Archives

Before attempting to use archival records the researcher should familiarize himself with some of the peculiarities inherent in that type of material.[2]

Manuscript records, as distinct from published volumes, require considerable preliminary study, as well as special handling, because under normal conditions collections of manuscripts can be catalogued only in general form; in fact, it is rarely possible to obtain for groups of manuscripts the precise subject classification one finds for books.

Great care should be exercised in using archival material, since in most cases the records are unique and if mutilated or lost may be irreplaceable. In view of the fact that records are usually not permanently bound, close attention should be paid to their original order and arrangement when used. Any disturbance in their original arrangement will invalidate the finding aids and result in great loss of research time. Like the "stack privilege" in the library, the privilege of using archival records is a valuable one. It should not be abused.

Ordinarily records are stored in an archive as they were in the original depository. Hence to use them it is necessary normally to

<hr>

[2] One of the best works on the general subject is Hilary Jenkinson and F. W. Maitland, *A Manual of Archival Administration* (London, 1937).

employ the same indexes and finding media as were used by the personnel who originally serviced them. This rule is not true of small collections of personal papers but, except for these groups and for occasional collections of great historical importance, archival and manuscript collections will not be indexed independently by the archival agency.

Obviously, to search records as they were searched by the agency that created them requires that the researcher be reasonably familiar with the organization of the agency whose records he is using. Thus, he will be able to determine where he should find records about a particular subject by knowing what subordinate division did that particular work; moreover, he should also be familiar with the recordkeeping methods used at various times by various agencies concerned.

The collections of original records and documents are vast and are located in a number of different depositories. They form the actual substance of a majority of all primary source material. Many unofficial documents bearing upon the military are to be found in the Library of Congress. In general, official military records are located in three principal agencies of custody, depending on the date span of the materials: The National Archives for the period 1776–1939; The Adjutant General's three records centers from 1940 to 1945; and partly in The Adjutant General's records centers and partly in the originating offices from 1946 to the present.[3] These cut-off dates are only a broad guide, and there are numerous exceptions with respect to a number of Army branches and agencies. Officials in The Adjutant General's Office should be consulted for specific information as to any given collection or category of documents. The following paragraphs are only a general guide to the major depositories and their contents, with representative examples of the more important collections.

Manuscript Division of Library of Congress

The Manuscript Division of the Library of Congress contains the private papers of most of the Presidents of the United States and of many important military figures. The Library has issued guides to its manuscript holdings, but these are out of date. It would be advisable for a prospective researcher to request information concerning material on any particular subject.

National Archives

Permanently valuable governmental records no longer needed by a Federal agency in the transaction of business are generally filed in the National Archives. Some of the records there date from the late 18th century; others are of very recent date.

---

[3] For further detail see AR 345–224.

The National Archives has issued a *Guide,* the latest edition of which appeared in 1948. In the *Guide* are listed the various record groups. For each record group there is given a very short administrative history of the governmental agency or part of an agency that created the records in the group. For example, the Federal Trade Commission would be considered a record group while in a large department, such as the Department of the Army, The Adjutant General's Office would be considered a separate record group. Following the administrative history of the record group there is a brief description of the records and of their cubic footage.

In addition there are prepared *Preliminary Inventories,* which in the main follow the pattern of the *Guide* but discuss at greater length the contents of the holdings in a particular record group—their beginning and terminal dates, cubic footage, and method of arrangement. If there is an index available to the records, it is noted. National Archives *Preliminary Inventories* available in 1955 include—

Preliminary Inventory of the Records of the:

Chemical Warfare Service
Council of National Defense
Office of the Paymaster General
Civilian Conservation Corps
Adjutant General's Office
Selective Service System, 1940–47
United States War Ballot Commission
Select Committee of the House of Representatives on Post-War Military Policy, 1944–46
Military Affairs Committee of the House of Representatives Relating to an Investigation of the War Department, 1934–36.

The *Guide* may be purchased from the Government Printing Office and the *Preliminary Inventories* are available upon request at the National Archives.

Military Libraries

There are a number of official Army libraries devoted almost exclusively to military works. For Army personnel these libraries constitute the most readily accessible depositories of source material dealing with military problems. Army libraries also have exchange privileges that make it possible to gain access to the holdings of other libraries. The more important military libraries are: Department of the Army, Pentagon, Washington 25, D. C.; National War College, Fort Lesley J. McNair, D. C.; Army War College, Carlisle Barracks, Pa.; Armed Forces Staff College, Norfolk 11, Va.; Command and General Staff College, Fort Leavenworth, Kans.;

United States Military Academy, West Point, N. Y.; and the libraries of the various service schools.

State, Local, and Special Collections

Many depositories throughout the United States have collections rich in military materials. Among the more significant are: American Antiquarian Society, Worcester, Mass.; Boston Athenaeum, Boston, Mass.; William L. Clements Library, Ann Arbor, Mich.; Archives of Maryland, Baltimore, Md.; Virginia Historical Society, Richmond, Va.; Georgia Historical Society, Savannah, Ga.; Massachusetts Historical Society, Boston, Mass.; New York Historical Society, New York, N. Y.; Historical Society of Pennsylvania, Philadelphia, Pa.; Wisconsin State Historical Society, Madison, Wis.; Henry E. Huntington Library, San Marino, Calif.; Chicago Historical Society, Chicago, Ill.; Illinois State Historical Library, Springfield, Ill.; Hoover Library, Stanford University, Stanford, Calif.; Franklin D. Roosevelt Library, Hyde Park, N. Y.; University Libraries of Harvard, Yale, Princeton, Columbia, University of Texas, Duke University, University of North Carolina; and the departments of archives and history of the various states. Guides are available for many of these collections. For additional information, consult *Historical Societies in the U. S. and Canada: A Handbook,* ed. C. C. Crittenden and Doris Godard (Washington, 1944).

American Military Organization and Records

Major Changes in the Military Records System

Effective research in American military history requires some knowledge of military records and the manner in which they were indexed and filed during the past. A brief description of some of the various systems that have been used follows:

The "Book Period" 1800–1889. During this period incoming correspondence was registered and outgoing letters were copied in large record books. Orders, descriptive rolls, musters, marches, changes of station, as well as other important information, were also copied therein. These books were supplemented by a "document file," consisting of the originals of letters received, orders, reports, and related papers.

The "Record Card Period" 1890–1917. During this period information formerly entered in record books was copied on large cards.

The "Decimal Classification Period" 1917 to the present. Since 1917, incoming papers and copies of outgoing correspondence have been arranged in one file and classified by subject according to the War Department (Department of the Army) decimal classification scheme.

Types of Historical Records

Regimental Records. These records are divided into two basic groups. The first group consists of muster rolls, which were periodic listings for pay purposes. Hence, they usually give little information beyond names, dates of enlistment and of last payment, together with a notation of important facts such as wounds, deaths, illnesses, desertions, discharges, and so forth.

The second group of regimental records, descriptive rolls, were in certain cases the original muster-in rolls; these furnish much more information, including age, place of birth, marital status, civilian occupation, personal description, and sometimes a brief individual service history. During the book period descriptive rolls were copied into the regimental books and maintained as continuing records.

Other important regimental rolls include morning reports and strength returns, proceedings of general and special courts-martial, inspection reports, operational records such as field orders and journals, and combat reports.

Post Records. These records consist of strength returns, orders which are sometimes filed with the strength returns, and records of events (otherwise filed with strength returns).

Brigade, Division, Corps, and Army Records. These are generally of the same type as the regimental records but they usually become progressively more elaborate in the higher echelons of command.

Military Territorial Command Records. Since 1813, the United States has been divided into geographical areas for purposes of military command. The resulting territorial subdivisions, as well as their designations, have been changed from time to time. For changes in boundaries, composition, and commanders of geographical areas previous to 1880, see Raphael P. Thian, *Military Geography of the United States, 1813–1880.*

American Military Records and Collections

Records in National Archives

These records vary so much in character and have emanated from so many different sources, some of which also underwent changes, that it is impossible to cover them all in this text. The researcher should consult the National Archives *Guide* for more detailed information. The date span of these records is generally 1814–1939. It should be noted that many of the records, particularly those on discipline, morale, quality of leadership at lower echelons, character of soldiers, judicial procedure, and the nature of military justice, have never been exploited.

Collections in the Records of The Adjutant General's Office

The Adjutant General's Office, Department of the Army, is the principal custodian of current original records and documents. The major collections are maintained and administered by the Departmental Records Branch, and are located at the Federal Records Center, Alexandria, Va.

In general, the date span of the records in this depository covers the period 1939 through 1945. Original records and documents which have not been retired to the Departmental Records Branch are maintained in the office, agency, or headquarters of origin. There are many individual exceptions to the cut-off dates of various collections, and the officials of the Departmental Records Branch should be consulted for exact information. This branch maintains custody of all headquarters records of all branches, agencies, and component organizations of the War Department and the Army. These records are organized and arranged in various collections, including classified and unclassified material. Among the outstanding collections are the following groups:

Records of the Office of the Secretary of War.

Records of the divisions of the General Staff, of which the War Plans Division and Operations Division collection are of particular importance.

Records of the Office of the Chief of Staff.

Records of the Arms, Services, and Branches.

Combat records of World War II, including combat operations reports, journals, periodic reports, after action reports, and other records, from army group to regiments and separate battalions.

Combined British-American records, World War II, which include the records of Allied Force Headquarters, Africa and Mediterranean Theater of Operations (AFHQ); Supreme Headquarters, Allied Expeditionary Forces, European Theater of Operations (SHAEF); General Headquarters, Southwest Pacific (GHQ SWPA); and Southeast Asia Command (SEAC), in either original form or in microfilm.

Records of the major commands under the War Department reorganization of 1942, including those of the Army Ground Forces and Army Service Forces.

War Crimes records, including those pertaining to the Nuremburg and Tokyo trials.

Collection of captured German documents, including a wide variety of materials, mostly in the original, some of which have been translated.

The records of the Army Air Forces have been transferred to the custody of the U. S. Air Force.

The Departmental Records Branch, Adjutant General's Office, maintains a variety of catalogues, inventories, and indexes to the various collections. Descriptive lists, inventories, and guides are constantly being prepared by that office.

Of special interest is the Historical Program File which comprises a large quantity of basic research materials relating largely to the technical services for use in the preparation of monographic studies. Most of the studies themselves are in the collections of the Office of the Chief of Military History.

Collections in Other Army Agencies, Washington, D. C.

In addition to records contained in agencies of The Adjutant General's office, others are maintained by Army agencies in the Washington area. Three of these are as follows:

Engineer records, comprising special categories of materials, in the custody of the Office of the Chief of Engineers, are located at Gravelly Point, Va., and some at Fort Belvoir, Va. These supplement the engineer records in the custody of The Adjutant General's Office.

Records of The Surgeon General's Office which include special categories of materials maintained in the custody of the Office of The Surgeon General. There are also valuable historical materials in the Army Medical Library.

Records of the Office of the Selective Service System which include all the central records relating to the draft in World War II, maintained in the custody of the Director of the Selective Service System.

Military Collections Outside Washington, D. C.

Records Centers of The Adjutant General. In addition to the collections maintained in The Adjutant General's Office, Washington and Alexandria, major depositories of important Army records and documents are located in the Records Centers at St. Louis, Mo., and Kansas City, Mo. The Army Records Center in St. Louis contains large collections relating to individual personnel matters, demobilized personnel records, financial accounts, and all Army contract records. The date span varies. Some demobilized personnel records cover the period from 1913 to date. The Records Center in Kansas City maintains custody of table of organization unit records for all overseas commands and some of the interior commands, including those of World War II; and headquarters records of all zone of the interior commands, including posts, corps areas, service commands, and their subordinate organizations and units.

Information concerning The Adjutant General's depositories may be obtained by addressing correspondence as follows:

Commanding Officer, Army Records Center, TAGO, 9700 Page Boulevard, St. Louis 14, Mo.

Commanding Officer, Kansas City Records Center, 601 Hardesty Avenue, Kansas City 24, Mo.

United States Military Academy, West Point, N. Y. The Academy records include post orders, and superintendents' and adjutants' letter books. They also include a variety of cadet records from which the Military Academy career of any of the graduates can be recreated. The personal records of graduates starting with the class of 1918 have been transferred to the Kansas City Records Center.

The records of the Academy also include some personal papers and memorabilia of distinguished graduates and government officials. With few exceptions these materials are related to the history of the Military Academy and of the Army.

Additional Collections. In addition to the above major depositories outside Washington there are numerous others of lesser and specialized importance. A few examples are the ordnance records located at the Aberdeen Proving Ground, Aberdeen, Md.; the records located at the Engineer Historical Section, Baltimore, Md.; and the Signal Corps Photograph and Film Collection, located at Long Island, N. Y. The Historical Records Section, Departmental Records Branch, Adjutant General's Office, should be consulted for complete coverage of these special collections, their contents, and location.

Published Documentary Materials

Reports of Agencies of the Military Establishment

These include the *Annual Reports of the Secretary of War* (after 1947 *Annual Reports of the Secretary of Army*) which contain the annual reports of the Chief of Staff and sections providing statistical reports on the strength, composition, organization, and distribution of the Army. These reports are brief, but are highly valuable as a guide to problems, policy, major events and developments, and changes within the Military Establishment that can be further explored in detail in the original records and documents. Of a like nature are reports of the Secretaries of Defense, Navy, and Air Force. The *Annual Reports of the Militia Bureau* (after 1933 *Annual Reports of the National Guard Bureau*) are a primary source for the organization, strength, distribution, problems, policies, and administration of the National Guard. Of equal value are the annual reports of various chiefs of branches, such as those of the Chief of Engineers, The Surgeon General, and the Chief of Coast Artillery. Some of these, such as the reports of The Surgeon General, were issued in printed form. Others were mimeographed for limited distribution.

General and Special Statutes Relating to the Army

Noteworthy examples include the National Defense Act of 1916, whose provisions formed the basis of the organization and structure of the Army at the end of World War I, and the National Defense Act of 1920 and its subsequent amendments, which provided the permanent basis of the Military Establishment's framework and organization to the present time. The edition of January 1945 includes all amendments to that date, together with all cognate acts and the sources of all provisions in effect. This composite statute is an indispensable source for the basic organization and structure of the Army. Examples of collected legislation pertaining to this period are *Laws Relating to National Defense Enacted by the 76th Congress,* comp. E. Lewis (Washington, 1941), and *Laws Relating to National Defense Enacted by the 77th Congress,* comp. E. Lewis (Washington, 1943). Other specific military legislation may be found in *United States Statutes at Large* for the years covered by this period.

Congressional Documents

Documents relating to Congressional proceedings on military affairs provide a valuable source of historical material. Debates in the Senate and House on military questions are printed in the *Congressional Record.* Of special importance are the published *Hearings* before the Committees on Military Affairs and (subsequent to January 1947) the Armed Services Committees of both houses of Congress. The *Hearings* before the Committee on Appropriations which record proceedings on the Army appropriation bills each year are of particular value. Numerous special committees of Congress have investigated incidents, affairs, or events of a military nature. The hearings before these committees constitute important source material for the historian. An example of this type is the *Hearings* before the Joint Committee on the Investigation of the Pearl Harbor Attack.

Army Regulations

Army Regulations, together with their revisions and changes, provide indispensable source material for tracing the history of Army organization, administration, and operations.

War Department Circulars, Bulletins

These supplement the various regulations and provide equally valuable material on the organization, administration, and operations of the Army. For example, War Department Circular 59, 1942, contains the specific provisions of the War Department reorganization of that year.

War Department General and Special Orders

These orders also contain much material relating to the administration and operations of the Army. In addition they provide important biographical data, since some general and most special orders relate to individuals.

Training Literature, Regulations, and Manuals

These are indispensable for tracing the history and development of training principles, doctrine, and techniques.

Miscellaneous Documents

In addition to the major categories mentioned above, numerous miscellaneous types of official documents provide a further body of source material for the historian. Such documents include staff regulations, bulletins, Executive orders, technical manuals, technical bulletins, tables of organization and equipment, tables of allowances, published reports of board proceedings, and various other papers.

Unpublished Documentary Materials

General

In addition to the several categories of official documents listed above there is a steadily increasing number of works relating to World War II. Much of this unpublished material is in the custody of various agencies of the Military Establishment. In general it includes unpublished studies, monographs, reports, and other papers in the several higher schools of the Army, as well as similar materials in the collections of the Office of the Chief of Military History.

The National War College Studies and Monographs

Many individual studies and committee reports on politico-military subjects have been prepared by students representing principally the Army, Navy, Air Force, and State Departments. In addition there are on file lectures by visiting experts of our political, military, economic, and psycho-social aspects of our national and international policies. This material cannot be considered as portraying the official attitude of the Government or the Departments concerned, since one of the prime purposes of the college curriculum is to encourage breadth of thought and consideration of problems by the students.

Army Industrial College (Industrial College of the Armed Forces) Studies and Monographs

From its establishment in 1924 to its suspension in December 1941, studies, monographs, reports, and lectures of the Army Industrial College were, with few exceptions, prepared in manuscript form. These documents, lodged in the Library of the College, are available for study. After the reopening of the College in 1943, policy with reference to materials was revised. Under the new policy all major materials are published in regular series by category and chronologically. They are deposited in the library of the Industrial College of the Armed Forces. Basic series of publications maintained by the College include—Research and Miscellaneous Reports (Code "R"); Lectures (Code "L"); Seminars (Code "S"); and Student Reports (Code "SR").

Army War College Studies and Monographs

Studies, monographs, analyses, and reports on a wide variety of subjects relating to strategy, to high organizational, administrative, and staff questions, and to other topics of importance and interest, have been prepared by groups of student officers and by members of the Army War College faculty and staff. They are especially valuable for the bibliographical leads they contain. The college maintains an excellent index and catalogue of subjects.

Command and General Staff College (School) Studies

Many studies, monographs, reports, and such papers, relating to tactical, logistical, staff, and administrative subjects on the division, corps, and army levels, have been prepared by student officers in the college. There are also special studies by faculty members. The college maintains an excellent index of subjects. A periodic list of subjects is published.

Service Schools Studies and Monographs

The schools of the arms and services have important holdings of historical material in the form of individual monographs or studies and committee reports prepared by students and members of the staff and faculty. These holdings at each of the schools pertain largely to the arm or service concerned.

Guides to Library Materials

Guides to Doctoral Dissertations Accepted by American Universities.— Nos. 1 through 16. Compiled for the Association of Research Libraries. New York 1933–.

Guides to Reference Works

Ireland, Norma O. *An Index to Indexes: a Subject Bibliography to Published Indexes.* Boston, 1942.

Mudge, Isadore G. *Guide to Reference Books.* 6th ed.; Chicago 1936.

Shores, Louis. *Basic Reference Books: An Introduction to the Evaluation, Study and Use of Reference Materials.* Chicago, 1939.

Guides to Magazines

Gregory, Winifred (ed.). *Union List of Serials in the United States and Canada.* 2d ed.; New York, 1943. This union list catalogue shows where copies of over 70,000 different magazines of all periods may be found in United States and Canadian libraries. It is indispensable to one working with older magazines. It does not index the articles in the magazines.

Magazine Subject Index, 1907–. Boston, 1908–. This magazine index is intended as a supplement to *Poole's Index* and the *Reader's Guide.* It specializes in historical articles, particularly those on local history.

Poole's Index to Periodical Literature, 1802–1881. Rev. ed.; Boston, 1891. 2 vols. and 5 vols. of supplements to include 1906. About 590,000 articles from 470 American and English periodicals are listed. Nonfictional material, including reviews of books, is indexed by subject only. For a fuller description of this and other periodical indexes and guides, see Mudge, *op. cit.* In order to locate a magazine referred to in the index use the *Union List* mentioned above.

Public Affairs Information Service Bulletin (PAIS). New York, 1914–. (weekly)

Reader's Guide to Periodical Literature, 1900–. New York, 1905–. This is a modern cumulative magazine index, kept up to date monthly. Articles are listed under author, title, and subject when necessary. In addition, the Wilson Co. publishes other magazine indexes of a more specialized nature.

Wilson, H. W. Co. *International Index to Periodicals.* New York, 1907–.

Guides to Newspapers

Because of the immense number of items to be covered, newspaper indexes are quite rare. The Historical Records Survey, Works Progress Administration, prepared topical indexes for a number of newspapers. Some work of a similar nature has been done by other agencies. A list of the newspapers so covered is given in H. O. Brayer, "Preliminary Guide to Indexed Newspapers in the United States," reprinted from the *Mississippi Valley Historical Review,* September 1946 (Vol. 33, No. 2).

Brigham, Clarence S. "Bibliography of American Newspapers, 1690–1820," in the American Antiquarian Society *Proceedings* (Vols. 23–37, with some volumes omitted). This gives historical sketches of newspapers published in the period, with frequency and dates and a checklist of copies to be found in various libraries in the United States. For other checklists of early newspapers see Mudge, *op. cit.*

Gregory, Winifred. *American Newspapers, 1821–1936.* New York, 1937. This is a new union list of newspaper holdings of nearly 5,700 depositories including private collections. It attempts to cover all United States newspapers published in the period. The Library of Congress has also published checklists of 18th century American newspapers and of foreign newspapers among its holdings.

New York Times Index, 1913–. New York, 1913–. This is a carefully made index to items appearing in the *Times.* It includes cross reference and brief synopses of many items.

Slauson, A. B. (comp.). *Check List of American Newspapers in the Library of Congress.* Washington, 1901. It lists newspapers by states and towns and gives a historical sketch of each with its frequency and dates of publication.

Guides to Archives and Manuscript Collections

National Archives *Guide to the Records in the National Archives.* Washington, 1948. This guide is indispensable to the researcher in American military history. The National Archives has also prepared a series of inventories of the Army records it holds.

Library of Congress

Fitzpatrick, John C. *Handbook of Manuscripts in the Library of Congress.* Washington, 1918. The collections are listed alphabetically by principal name or subject, with an index for every name and many subjects. The collection is also generally broken down into small groups of papers with the dates and topics of each.

Garrison, Curtiss W. *List of Manuscript Collections in the Library of Congress to July 1931.* Washington, 1932. It includes material in the *Handbook* plus additions received to July 1931 but in less detail. Arrangement of collections is by period.

Powell, C. Percy. *List of Manuscript Collections in the Library of Congress July 1931 to 1938.* Washington, 1939. It contains additions since the Garrison *List* with much the same arrangement. Detailed finding media to all its collections exist in the Manuscript Division, Library of Congress, where the documents listed in the above three references are housed.

Manuscript Collections

Griffin, Grace G. (comp.). *A Guide to Manuscripts Relating to American History in British Depositories, Reproduced for the Division of Manuscripts, Library of Congress.* Washington, 1946. The Carnegie Institution has issued a series of other guides to manuscript collections in the United States and foreign countries that contain material bearing on American history.

Historical Records Survey, Works Progress Administration. *Guide to Depositories of Manuscript Collections in the United States.* Washington, 1938; arranged by state. It lists the principal historical manuscript depositories in 18 states with their holdings. It also lists guides to these holdings where available. The survey has not been completed. Only California, Florida, Illinois, Iowa, Louisiana, Massachusetts, Michigan, Minnesota, Missouri, Nebraska, New Hampshire, New Jersey, New York, North Carolina, Oregon, Pennsylvania, Tennessee, and Wisconsin are covered.

Library of Congress. *Checklist of Collections of Personal Papers in Historical Societies, University and Public Libraries, and Other Learned Institutions in the United States.* Washington, 1918. This is the first important attempt to list the collections of "personal papers" in the United States. Principal names or subjects are listed alphabetically with a detailed rearrangement by periods which is in effect an index.

Library of Congress. *Manuscripts in Public and Private Collections in the United States.* Washington, 1924. An enlargement of the above *Checklist,* arranged by states with a detailed index.

Commercially published guides to specific collections are available in increasing number and excellence and may be secured from depositories concerned.

Guides to Published Government Documents

General Documents

Boyd, Anna M. *U. S. Government Publications as Sources of Information for Libraries.* 3d ed.; New York, 1941.

Clark, Edith E. *Guide to the Use of United States Government Documents.* Boston, 1918.

Schmeckebier, L. F. *Government Publications and Their Use.* Washington, 1936.

Wyer, James I., Jr. *United States Government Documents, Federal, State, and City.* Rev. ed.; Chicago, 1933. This guide is designed to assist in the use of government publications.

Federal Documents

Ames, John G. *Comprehensive Index to the Publications of the United States Government, 1881–1893.* Washington, 1905. This index bridges the gap between Poore's *Catalogue* and the *Document Catalogue.*

National Archives. *Federal Records of World War II.* Washington, 1950. 2 vols. "These two volumes, entitled *Federal Records of World War II,* are intended to serve as a guide to materials that will be useful for research, particularly in the planning and administration of national defense activities. They are by no means to be thought of as providing a complete description of the records."

Poore, Benjamin P. *Descriptive Catalogue of the Government Publications of the United States, September 5, 1774–March 4, 1881.* Washington, 1885. The catalogue is arranged chronologically with a general but insufficiently detailed index. The full title, author, date and location of each document is given, with a brief summary of its contents.

U. S. Superintendent of Documents. *Catalogue of the Public Documents of Congress and of all Departments of the Government of the United States.* Washington, 1893—. This is the permanent and complete catalogue of government publications for the modern period, comprehensively indexed. It is usually called *Document Catalogue.*

State and Local Documents

Bowker, Richard R. *State Publications.* New York, 1899–1909. 4 vols. It is not up to date but helpful in locating state documents published prior to 1909.

Thorpe, Francis N. *Federal and State Constitutions, Colonial Charters and Other Organic Laws of the States, Territories, and Colonies* . . . . Washington, 1909. 7 vols. This is a comprehensive collection of basic legislation governing state military forces.

U. S. Library of Congress. *Monthly Check-List of State Publications.* Washington, 1910–. This is a current bibliography of official state documents maintained since 1909. Arranged by states and indexed broadly by subject.

For additional document catalogues and checklists, including those of foreign governments, consult Mudge, *op. cit.*

Guides to Maps

American Geographical Society. *Books and Maps.* New York, 1946.

British War Office. *Catalog of Maps.* Published by the Directorate of Military Survey.

Claussen, Martin P., and Herman R. Friis. *Descriptive Catalogue of Maps Published by Congress.* Washington, 1941.

Hammond, C. S. & Co. *Maps by Hammond.* New York, current.

Harrison, Richard E. *Look at the World.* The Fortune Atlas for World Strategy. New York, 1944.

LeGear, Clara E. *U. S. Atlases, a List of National, State, County, City, and Regional Atlases in the Library of Congress.* Washington, 1950.

National Archives: The Cartographic Branch of the National Archives administers some 850,000 different maps, ranging from 1787 to the present, that have been selected for preservation because of their permanent evidential or informational value. The maps relate primarily to the United States, dealing with its geography, exploration, history, settlement, economic development, and administration, but there are also included maps of other parts of the world that have been involved in the country's foreign relations in war and peace.

National Geographic Society. *A List of Maps Produced by the National Geographic Society.* Washington, current.

Paullin, Charles O., and John K. Wright. *Atlas of Historical Geography of the United States.* New York, 1932.

Phillips, Philip L. *List of Maps in America in the Library of Congress.* Washington, 1901.

———. *Geographical Atlases in the Library of Congress.* Washington, 1909–20. 4 vols.

Rand McNally & Co. *Catalogs of Atlases and Maps.* Chicago, current.

Thiele, Walter. *Official Map Publications.* Chicago, 1938.

U. S. Department of Agriculture. *Aerial Photography Status Maps.* Washington, Revised 1 January 1949.

U. S. Air Forces. *Catalog of Aeronautical Charts and Related Publications.* 8th ed.; Washington.

U. S. Army Map Service. *General Map Catalog.* Washington, current; *Indexes for Selected Map Coverage.* Washington, 1941–43; and *Index to Topographic Quadrangles.* Washington.

U. S. Department of Commerce. *Catalog of Nautical Charts and Related Publications, Coast and Geodetic Survey.* Washington.

U. S. Department of the Interior. *Catalog of Publications of Geological Survey.* Includes maps. Washington, current.

U. S. Lake Survey. *Catalog of Charts.* Detroit.

Winterbotham, Harold S. J. L. *A Key to Maps.* 2d ed.; London and Glasgow, 1939.

Wright, John K., and Elizabeth T. Platt. *Aids to Geographical Research.* New York, 1947.

Historical Atlases

Hammond, C. S. *March of Civilization.* New York, 1950.

Muir, Ramsey. *Historical Atlas.* New York, 1927.

———. *Philips New School Atlas of Universal History.* London, 1935.

Shephert, William R. *Historical Atlas.* New York, 1929.

——— . *Historical Atlas.* (Rev. ed.) Pikesville, Md., 1955.

Military Museums and Collections: How to Use Them

General

Military history written from documents alone often tends to lack both accuracy and color. A knowledge of how things looked, how they operated, what they weighed, and so forth is essential to the complete story. Oftentimes such knowledge can be acquired only by a careful and critical examination of pictures, photographs, and artifacts. Such items, other than those of current interest, are normally found only in historical museums. Thus it is important that a military writer know something about these institutions in the United States.

Broadly, American military museums fall into three groups: those maintained by the military services; those maintained by civil agencies of the Federal Government; and, finally, museums operated by private agencies or by states, municipalities, etc. In all three types existing collections vary from excellent to poor, with most in the latter category. Therefore the researcher should not put too much dependence upon data included on labels. Even the artifacts and pictures should be examined every bit as critically as documents and published sources.

A listing of historical museums as of 1944 can be found in *Historical Societies in the United States and Canada: A Handbook,* published by the American Association for State and Local History.

Museums Maintained by the Armed Forces

The Army's most important museum is located at the United States Military Academy at West Point, N. Y. Although many of its objects relate solely to the Academy, the Museum does include a large amount of material illustrating the history of the Army at large. The Ordnance Corps maintains an excellent collection of older shoulder weapons at Springfield Armory, Springfield, Mass., and an equally important collection of modern weapons at Aberdeen Proving Grounds, Md. Several smaller Army museums deserve mention: the collection at Rock Island, Ill.; the Patton Museum at Fort Knox, Ky.; and the Artillery School Museum at Fort Sill, Okla.

The Navy's principal collection of historic objects is at the United States Naval Academy at Annapolis, Md. The Truxtun-Decatur Naval Museum, located in Washington, D. C., contains a small but periodically changing exhibit. This museum is maintained by the Naval Historical Foundation, an unofficial society, but some assistance is derived from the Navy. The Marine Corps has a small collection of objects associated with its history at Quantico, Va. The U. S. Air Force has a technical museum at Wright-Patterson Air Force Base, Dayton, Ohio.

Museums Maintained by Civil Agencies of the United States

In the second category are two agencies: the U. S. National Museum in Washington and the National Park Service with museums located throughout the country. The National Museum devotes several halls of the Arts and Industries Building to military and naval exhibits while the Air Museum contains items related to the history of military aviation in this country. The National Park Service maintains 26 systematic museums on battlefields. The more important are as follows:

Antietam National Battlefield Site, Md.
Appomattox Courthouse National Historical Monument, Va.
Castillo de San Marcos National Monument, Fla.
Chickamauga-Chattanooga National Military Park, Tenn.

390016 O - 56 - 5

Custer Battlefield National Monument, Mont.
Fort Laramie National Monument, Wyo.
Fort McHenry National Monument, Md.
Fort Pulaski National Monument, Ga.
Fort Raleigh National Historic Site, N. C.
Fort Washington, Md.
Fredericksburg and Spotsylvania National Military Park, Va.
Gettysburg National Military Park, Pa.
Guilford Courthouse National Military Park, N. C.
Kennesaw Mountain National Military Park, Ga.
Kings Mountain National Military Park, S. C.
Lincoln Museum, Washington, D. C.
Manassas National Battlefield Park, Va.
Morristown National Historical Park, N. J.
Petersburg National Military Park, Va.
Richmond National Battlefield Park, Va.
San Juan National Historic Site, P. R.
Saratoga National Historical Park, N. Y.
Scotts Bluff National Monument, Nebr.
Shiloh National Military Park, Tenn.
Vicksburg National Military Park, Miss.

Although small, these museums are among the most up to date in the United States. Each confines its attention to the battlefield or area where it is located.

Museums Maintained by Other Agencies

Fort Ticonderoga Museum, located in the restored fort on Lake Champlain, is the outstanding military collection in the United States not maintained by federal funds. In addition to this, however, there are over a thousand local museums and historical societies in the United States whose small and often haphazard collections contain some military objects. Among these the more significant are the Essex Institute in Salem, Mass.; the New York Historical Society and Museum of the City of New York, in New York City; and the Confederate Museum and the Battle Abbey in Richmond, Va.

Use of Military Museums and Collections

Before visiting a museum for research, it is usually advisable to communicate with the institution and to ascertain the hours it will be open. This may save precious time. Only the larger institutions have facilities for photographing objects, and very few are able to furnish the serious student with background data on exhibits.

Military Art

During the Mexican and Civil Wars minor projects were undertaken. In World War II and subsequent thereto much more effort has been devoted to military art. There are, however, no outstanding collections of military art in America, but rather a wide dispersion in numerous galleries and private collections. Most of the official art is displayed in the Pentagon and at various Army installations throughout the United States

The Office of the Chief of Military History, Washington, D. C., has considerable information on American military art and related matters, and is prepared to render assistance to military students and historians.

The Company of Military Collectors & Historians, Washington, D. C., is a private nonprofit, educational institution, devoted to the study and dissemination of information about military history, uniforms, weapons, insignia, and equipage. It publishes the magazine *Military Collector & Historian.*

Historical Films

The motion picture with sound recordings has become an important aid to instruction in history as in all other fields, but the military services have not always made the very best possible use of this medium. This is reflected in the quality and coverage of available films.

Commercial firms, foundations, and educational institutions have produced a number of films showing military events of our earlier wars. Many of these films have been produced without adequate research and, therefore, are not entirely accurate. The military services themselves have produced a large number of historical films since 1917, but much of this material remains inadequately integrated into the broader history of a particular campaign or war. In spite of these inherent deficiencies, however, many existing films can be used advantageously in military instruction. The service films also are of great value to researchers and historians concerned with events of a particular period, because they can glean from them an understanding of the conditions that existed at the time.

The following publications include a list of films, television recordings, and filmstrips of a historical nature:

DA Pamphlet 108–1, *Index of Army Motion Pictures, Television Recordings, and Filmstrips.*

Krahn, Frederic A. ed., *Educational Film Guide* (with annual supplements) (11th ed.; New York, 1953).

CHAPTER IV
RESEARCH AND WRITING

General

Historical works of greatest value in military education should go beyond a simple account of past military operations or activities. They should include a critical analysis of the facts, the determination of conclusions, and, if possible, the lessons to be learned from the account. According to Clausewitz, such writing should follow three steps:

First, the historical investigation and determining of doubtful facts. This is properly historical research, and has nothing in common with theory.

Secondly, the tracing of effects to causes. This is the *real critical inquiry;* it is indispensable to theory, for everything which in theory is to be established, supported, or even merely explained, by experience can only be settled in this way.

Thirdly, the testing of the means employed. This is *criticism, properly speaking,* in which praise and censure is contained. This is where theory helps history, or rather, the teaching to be derived from it.[1]

Clausewitz elaborates on the last two steps as follows:

In these two last strictly critical parts of historical study, all depends on tracing things to their primary elements, that is to say, up to undoubted truths, and not, as is so often done, resting half-way, that is on some arbitrary assumption or supposition.

As respects the tracing of effect to cause, that is often attended with the insuperable difficulty that the real causes are not known. In none of the relations of life does this so frequently happen as in War, where events are seldom fully known, and still less motives, as the latter have been, perhaps purposely, concealed by the chief actor, or have been of such a transient and accidental character that they have been lost for history. For this reason critical narration must generally proceed hand in hand with historical investigation, and still such a want of connection between cause and effect will often present itself, that it does not seem justifiable to consider effects as the necessary results of known causes. Here, therefore, voids must occur, that is historical results which cannot be made use of for teaching. All that theory can demand is that the investigation should be rigidly conducted up to that point, and there leave off without drawing conclusions. A real evil

---

[1] Clausewitz, *op. cit.*, I, p. 130.

springs up only if the known is made perforce to suffice as an explanation of effects, and thus a false importance is ascribed to it.

Besides this difficulty, critical inquiry also meets with another great and intrinsic one, which is that the progress of events in War seldom proceeds from one simple cause, but from several in common, and that it therefore is not sufficient to follow up a series of events to their origin in a candid and impartial spirit, but that it is then also necessary to apportion to each contributing cause its due weight. This leads, therefore, to a closer investigation of their nature, and thus a critical investigation may lead into what is the proper field of theory.

The critical *consideration*, that is the testing of the means, leads to the question, Which are the effects peculiar to the means applied, and whether these effects are comprehended in the plans of the person directing? [2]

And then in commenting on the use of historical examples and the role of a military writer, Clausewitz summarized his views as follows:

It would be an immense service to teach the Art of War entirely by historical examples . . . ; but it would be full work for the whole life of a man, if we reflect that he who undertakes it must first qualify himself for the task by a long personal experience in actual War.

Whoever, stirred by ambition, undertakes such a task, let him prepare himself for his pious undertaking as for a long pilgrimage; let him give up his time, spare no sacrifice, fear no temporal rank or power, and rise above all feelings of personal vanity, of false shame, in order, according to the French code, to speak *the Truth, the whole Truth, and nothing but the Truth.*[3]

Steps in Research

Choosing a Subject

The wise choice of a subject is basic to the preparation of a good historical paper. Naturally the writer should possess a good general knowledge of the field in which he desires to work. To the professional officer, military history, especially that of the United States, should offer the most possibilities. Appropriate topics for military personnel can be found in "Suggested Thesis Subjects for Military Personnel Training in Civilian Institutions" which is distributed by the Office of the Chief of Military History, Department of the Army.

Once the general field has been determined, several considerations must be kept in mind in choosing a topic. It must possess unity and be sufficiently restricted in scope to be amenable to thorough investigation and detailed presentation. It must deal with a sig-

---

[2] *Ibid.*, pp. 130–31.
[3] *Ibid.*, p. 164.

nificant subject. It should investigate some new topic or add new knowledge to some known subject, since it is possible that the student can, by reexamination of old evidence coupled with a study of new evidence, correct errors or reinterpret matters that have been covered earlier. A study possessing these characteristics is called a monograph, and normally lies well within the scope of a student of a service school or college. Such a student should not attempt a comprehensive survey of a broad field, as works of this type usually require years, decades, or even a lifetime of research. Thus the beginner should avoid such topics as "The Allied Campaigns against Japan during World War II" or "Eisenhower's Campaigns in Northwest Europe," for these cannot be properly dealt with in less than several volumes. To write a comprehensive history of even one of the U. S. Army's campaigns in World War II requires at least three years' work by an experienced scholar with a great deal of assistance.

An example may best illustrate some of the steps involved in selection of a good topic. Assume that a hypothetical student officer served in a field artillery battalion in the Guadalcanal Campaign. Quickly deciding not to write on the entire campaign because it is too big and has already been covered by other writers, he elects to write a history of artillery operations, tentatively entitled "The Employment of Artillery in the Guadalcanal Campaign." His researches quickly disclose that the Guadalcanal Campaign embraced landings on Tulagi, Gavutu, Tenambogo, and the Russells, as well as on Guadalcanal. Deciding that a discussion of artillery in all these invasions would take too long, he cuts his subject down to "The Employment of Artillery on Guadalcanal, 7 August 1942–9 February 1943." But further researches disclose that antiaircraft artillery was employed, and he does not wish to involve himself and his readers in discussions involving radar, gunlaying directors, and remote-control systems. Further, he discovers that from time to time warships lay offshore giving fire support to the infantry. But he does decide to discuss, as much as possible, the Japanese employment of field artillery on Guadalcanal. Therefore, the topic he finally selects is "The Employment of Field Artillery on Guadalcanal, 7 August 1942–9 February 1943."

The Tentative Bibliography

As the writing of history is an organic process, no two subjects ever call for exactly the same steps in research. The steps listed below are merely suggestions and the student actually engaged in research will probably vary them in accordance with the needs of his subject. Concrete examples may best illustrate the early steps.

58

The hypothetical student, already referred to, has elected to write on "The Employment of Field Artillery on Guadalcanal, 7 August 1942–9 February 1943." From personal experience, from a study of newspapers and news magazines, and from general reading he has some familiarity with the nature and course of World War II in the Pacific. His professional military education and experience have made him familiar with military operations in general and have particularly qualified him to understand the nature, functions, and special problems of the field artillery.

Books

The officer's first step is to prepare a working bibliography to be used as a guide to sources to be consulted.[4] His first move is probably to consult the card catalogue of the library where he is working to find the books that deal with his subject. For most subjects, a formidable bibliography can be assembled by consulting author, title, and subject entries in the card catalogue. In assembling the bibliography, all relevant data concerning each book should be entered on separate cards or small slips of paper. This data includes names of authors or editors; the full title as it is printed on the book's title page; series title, if any; edition, if other than the first; the volume number and total number of volumes if more than one; and the name of the publisher, place published or publisher's home office, and date of publication. In case of a series, or a multivolume work, the initial and terminal years should be listed. If the series is not complete, the first year should be shown followed by a dash. Noting the library's call number on the card will save time if the book is needed again. However, the call number does not appear in the final bibliography included in the monograph. No more than one title should be entered on a single card; thus the cards can be later filed in logical order. In addition to the data listed above other bits of information that throw light on the value and authoritativeness of the book should be entered. Important among these are those items or parts that deal with his subject, the author's position if it qualified him as an authority, the scope of the book, and, finally, a brief evaluation by himself.[5]

The Bibliographical Card

In the case of the Guadalcanal Campaign, the military student would probably first examine the works produced in the Office of

---

[4] A fairly detailed treatment of the steps involved in preparing a tentative bibliography, but related to general history, may be found in Homer Carey Hockett, *Introduction to Research in American History* (2d ed.; New York, 1949), pp. 7ff.

[5] For methods of determining something about the quality of a book before reading see chapter II.

the Chief of Military History, Department of the Army, to determine if anything is available on his subject. Fortunately, he finds *Guadalcanal: The First Offensive* in the UNITED STATES ARMY IN WORLD WAR II series. The bibliographic card with the student's comment, should be something like this:

[call number]

(U. S. Department of the Army. Historical Division.)
Miller, John, jr.
Guadalcanal: The First Offensive (History of the War in Pacific: UNITED STATES ARMY IN WORLD WAR II, Kent Roberts Greenfield, General Editor)
Historical Division, Department of the Army
Washington, D. C., 1949.

. . . .

Books based on journals, action reports, war diaries, and JCS and OPD files. Covers USMC, U. S. Army, and Japanese ground opns; air and naval opns are summarized. Considerable attention to arty.

Once a few titles have been selected from the card catalogue and complete card entries filled out, as shown in the illustration, the researcher should examine the books. If any of the prospective titles prove valueless, they should be discarded at once.

Once the card catalogue has yielded all possible information, the bibliographies and footnotes of the books themselves should be studied to obtain additional titles and cards should be filled out on those items believed to be of interest.

Periodicals and Newspapers

Magazine and newspaper articles as well as government publications used in a study will be cited in footnotes and listed in the bibliography. The student will find in *Guadalcanal's* Bibliographical Note a list of useful magazine articles, several of which pertain to his subject. He should enter on a card the author's name, title of the article (in quotation marks), title of magazine (in italics), the volume and number, date, and the page reference if desired, although it is not absolutely necessary.

For articles in encyclopedias, the same form can be employed, but the number of the edition should be shown. When they do not fill entire volumes, articles in reports, and other papers published by scholarly organizations, can be listed like those in periodicals. In citing newspapers, give the name of the paper as it appears on the first page and the date of the issue. If the name of the city wherein the paper is published does not appear in the title, insert it in brackets. It is not necessary to show the page and column number of a newspaper article in a formal bibliography, but it will often save time to indicate them on a bibliographic entry.

U. S. Government Publications and Documents

Much of the writing in American military history must be done in primary source material using government documents and manuscripts. To do effective work, one must understand the various filing systems used by the Army throughout the years, and must know of the major depositories and the extent of materials located in them. If the subject chosen deals with a current or very recent problem, it is possible that all source material used may be of a primary nature.

Army Records

It is in U. S. Army records that the greatest difficulty in footnotes and bibliographic entries will probably be encountered, for there is no generally accepted practice for citing the manifold printed, typewritten, mimeographed, multilithed, and handwritten Army regulations, general orders, reports, planning papers, letters, memorandums, journals, radiograms, and messages that constitute U. S. Army documents. Appendix A of this *Guide* gives the system used by the Special Studies Division, Office of the Chief of Military History.

Records in the Department of the Army fall into four general categories: (1) letters, memorandums, and other communications; (2) archival material of a nonmanuscript character; (3) field records of military units and commands; and (4) records of the Joint and Combined Chiefs of Staff.

In the case of letters, memorandums, radiograms, and other communications that are usually filed in binders bearing numbers, the bibliographic entry should indicate the character of the documents, the general subject matter, the file or binder identification number, and the file location when consulted. Official abbreviations and short titles can be used for the tentative bibliography, but in the final bibliography only the most obvious abbreviations should be used. As in the case of books, the bibliographic entry should be followed by the researcher's addition of any data throwing light on the location and value of the collection. For example:

> Operations of the 25th Infantry Division
> Guadalcanal (2667) 325-11.5
> 17 December 1942–5 February 1943
> Filed in DRB, TAG.
>
> . . . .
>
> After the campaign Maj. Gen. J. Lawton Collins, CG, 25th Div., conducted a series of critiques on the action which were attended by practically all the division's officers and by key enlisted men from each unit. The record of these critiques, compiled as the 25th Division Operations, is a model of its kind.

The second category, archival material of a nonmanuscript character, presents few difficulties. It includes material like Army general orders, manuals, and Army regulations which can often be cited like books. The titles should not be italicized but placed in quotes. File locations need not be given.

The field records of military units and commands tend to overlap into the first category of letters, memos, and communications. It will be noted that the example cited above is derived from a field command. But there is a wide range of documents relating to combat that are submitted by field units and commands. The bibliographic entries for these should show the unit or command, character of the record or its title, or both, its date, and present file location. For example:

> GHQ, SWPA, G3 Journal (for a given period).
> Filed in Hist Rec Sec, Dept Rec Br,
> Admin Serv Div, AGO, Dept of the Army
> Federal Records Center, Alexandria, Va.
>
> . . . .
>
> Contains the secret, but not the top secret, entries, plans, orders, messages, and other papers.

The fourth category embraces materials which are not, strictly speaking, U. S. Army documents, but are the papers of the Joint and Combined Chiefs of Staff and subordinate committees which are essential to an understanding of the strategy of World War II. These documents fortunately are available in the Department of the Army.

Preliminary Reading for General Orientation

By this time the student will have made good progress on his bibliography and will have discarded what is obviously of little use. He will also have formed a general idea of the outline of his subject. These steps, although discussed separately, are not necessarily taken separately in practice. The assembly of a tentative bibliography, the appraising of the materials, and the preliminary reading are usually conducted almost concurrently.

Once it appears that the main elements of the bibliography have been assembled, the basic sources should be scanned to obtain a general outline of the events to be described. At this stage the author will not take many notes.

The Tentative Outline

When the preliminary reading has been completed and the general sequence of events has been determined, it is well to prepare a rough outline in order to focus the detailed, comprehensive reading that is to follow and to facilitate the taking of notes. For example, a study of *Guadalcanal* shows that the main aspects of field artillery employment included tactical support of infantry in offense and defense as well as counterbattery fire, and that the main problems of the field artillery were the difficulties of moving ammunition over rough jungle terrain, the selection of good positions, and the inadequacies of the available maps. These will constitute the main points of the outline and it should eventually be organized in such a way as to bring out clearly the interrelationship of the points.

It cannot be emphasized too strongly that this outline is tentative—it will be changed frequently as new facts emerge that change the relationship of the main points.

Taking Notes—Some General Considerations and Suggestions [6]

The first notes to be taken will probably come from the most general sources and will probably provide background material. Here the author will be dealing with items of common knowledge that do not require documentation. It will not be necessary, for example, to cite books to prove that the 1st Marine Division landed on Guad-

---

[6] For useful suggestions see Earl W. Dow, *Principles of a Note System for Historical Studies* (New York, 1924).

alcanal on 7 August 1942.   On the other hand, it is not unlikely that *Guadalcanal: The First Offensive* will need to be cited, for if the writer wishes to compare conclusions, or if he finds *Guadalcanal* in error, he will need to cite it.

As progress is made deeper into the subject, note-taking will increase, as will skill in taking notes.   As Hockett points out, the historian's instinct for the facts he needs, like the reporter's nose for news, develops with use.[7]   No precise rules can be formulated but a few general rules can be followed.   It is worse to take too few notes than too many, but the golden mean should be sought.   Only extremely important, exact, or particularly vivid passages need be copied verbatim.   Needless to say, any quoted passages must be quoted precisely as they appear in the original.   Let any errors stand but add [*sic*].   Interpolations that increase the meaning of a passage should also be placed in brackets (not parentheses), as "the 67th [Fighter Squadron] was fortunate."   When words are omitted, indicate the omission by three periods, but when they are omitted from the end of a sentence use four periods.   If a sentence is quoted and part of the succeeding material is omitted, place the period close to the last letter thus: "The fire devastated the vicinity of the water hole. . . . When the 1st Battalion attacked south against its objective over a route known to have been formerly strongly held by the enemy, it encountered only minor opposition."   Care should be taken to write notes in such a way that the material is kept within its context.   The meaning and intent of the original must be preserved.

Note taking is a mechanical as well as an intellectual process, and the mechanics are of vital importance.   The best and most convenient method involves a loose-leaf system.   Only through such a system can material be classified or rearranged.   The size used in the Office of Military History is five by eight inches.   Only one major item of information should be entered on a card.   In this way similar materials from widely separated sources studied at different times can be brought together.

As the facts or data are recorded, many comments and ideas regarding those facts will come to mind—points regarding their significance and accuracy, interpretations of their meaning and relationship to other facts, and other such generalizations.   These thoughts about the facts should be recorded at once on the same card rather than trusting to memory, for often a long time elapses between note taking and the actual writing of the paper.   To avoid later confusion, the author should clearly indicate the facts and his own comments.

---

[7] Hockett, *op. cit.*, p. 48.

Each note should have an appropriate topical heading and should contain the important bibliographical information. If a book, enter the author's name, the title, place and date of publication, and the page; if a magazine, give the author, title of article and magazine, volume, number, date, and page; if a military letter or memorandum, record the sender, recipient, date, and all relevant numbers such as AGO number, date–time–group, and CM–IN and CM–OUT numbers; if an order, report, or journal, enter the issuing headquarters, nature, title, date, and file location. For example:

Prep for arty, support of XIV Corps 1st Early Jan 43
Jan Offensive

25th Div Arty, Rpt Action Against Enemy, 10 Jan–10 Feb 43, p. 1. In Hist Rec Sec, Dept Rec Br, Admin Serv Div, AGO, Dept of Army

. . . .

Easy to select arty positions. Japanese lack of arty and air power enabled U. S. arty to ignore defilade, camouflage, and concealment. Could safely emplace wpns on fwd slopes of hill. Picked positions west of Lunga. (For exact positions see later notes from arty bn rpts.)

Arranging and Filing Notes

With the tentative outline completed, the student has some idea of how his material is to be organized. If he has arranged the outline into chapters, sections, and subsections, the notes themselves, with their topic headings as a guide can be arranged to conform to the outline. The degree of elaborateness of the system will of course depend on the elaborateness and intricacy of the subject matter. The notes themselves should be filed in a box, file drawer, or some convenient depository.

Evaluating Material

The evaluation of data, the application of critical standards to the sources, is one of the most significant and essential processes of historiography. Industrious, resourceful, meticulous, and aggressive research is basic to the writing of history, but it is wasted if the historian does not carefully evaluate his data.[8]   Through the processes of evaluation forgeries are exposed, anonymous writings are identified, false or erroneous statements are detected, bias is discovered, and eventually truth in relative if not in absolute form emerges. To repeat, historiography is an organic process.   The gathering of data and the criticism of data are not necessarily separate.   They normally will be conducted concurrently, although the criticism of data will continue until the final draft of the monograph is written.

One essential quality that all historians must possess is skepticism. Every source, no matter how respectable its origin, must be regarded as suspect until it has been tested and found valid.   There are innumerable examples in American history of reputable individuals who made serious errors in fact that either misled or puzzled historians.[9]   The fact that one's senses are easily deceived, that several eyewitnesses of an event will often honestly give completely different accounts is also well known.[10]   Aside from errors resulting from fading memories, ignorance, carelessness, and bad sensory perception, there are other equally serious false data in the sources, many of which arise from the self-interest of individuals or organizations. Official propaganda must always be suspect, as must the claims of individuals or units regarding their contributions to, say, a particular military campaign.   In these cases, the historian's ferreting out of errors is a task whose ease lies in inverse ratio to the degree of error.   The more false the statements in the source, the easier they are to detect.   Good (that is effective) propaganda, whether advancing the cause of a government, an infantry division, or a military commander is usually subtle; it avoids deliberate falsehoods.   It may mislead by subtle exaggeration or by suppression of pertinent facts.   The historian, therefore, must be constantly on the alert against misleading statements that derive from a multitude of causes.   As Allen Johnson has phrased it, "In historical studies doubt is the beginning of wisdom."[11]

In military operations in particular, evidence must be carefully weighed.   It is obvious that in the tension and confusion of battle the participants do not see, hear, or recollect with absolute clarity. Neither do they see from the same position or angle.   Few men engaged in battle have any clear conception of what is going on, although with modern developments in communications it appears that the fog of war has lessened, at least for unit commanders.

[8] For good discussions of the evaluation of data, see the following: Allen Johnson, *The Historian and Historical Evidence* (New York, 1926); Hockett, *op. cit.*, pp. 56–111; Charles V. Langlois and Charles Seignobos, *Introduction to the Study of History*, tr. G. Berry (New York, 1912), pp. 71–211; and A. P. Scott and J. L. Cate, *Syllabus and Problems for History 201, Introduction to Historical Method and Historiography* (Chicago, 1945), pp. 33–92.

[9] See, for example, Hockett, *op. cit.*, pp. 71–72; Johnson, *op. cit.*, pp. 40–52.

[10] See, for example, Johnson, *op. cit.*, pp. 24–33.

[11] *Ibid.*, p. 50.

Censorship, even though it is necessary for security or to bolster morale, leads to the suppression of facts, especially in news dispatches and communiques. Military reports submitted to higher headquarters are not always completely factual or truthful. Important facts may not be known at the time the report was rendered and errors and failures may be glossed over. Rumors of dubious origin spread rapidly and sometimes find their way into official reports.

External Criticism

External criticism involves those tests that seek to establish the authenticity of a particular document. It detects forgeries and false versions and identifies anonymous documents. It attempts to establish where, when, how, and by whom a document was written, for this knowledge is essential to the writing of history. This type of criticism is obviously one which the student of United States military history, especially recent history, seldom needs to employ. Forgeries and anonymous papers have been comparatively rare since the end of the 18th century. External criticism is used most often by historians of earlier periods who have developed elaborate skills to enable them to establish the origin of their sources. But as the average American military document is easily identified, internal analysis, comparison with other documents, textual criticism, emendations, and variant readings need not be discussed at length.[12]

Internal Criticism[13]

For the student or writer in American military history, internal criticism is, after his research, perhaps his most important single technique. Once a document has been identified, internal criticism is used to analyze the meaning of statements in the document and to determine their accuracy, trustworthiness, and sincerity. Internal criticism is also applied to data obtained by interview and correspondence.

Thus the first step in internal criticism is to determine, by careful reading and careful thinking, the exact meanings of the statements as intended by the authors. No statement should ever be torn out of its context. The propagandist's technique of quoting statements, or fragments of statements, out of their context is well known, and is abjured by all reputable writers. But one should be careful not to apply his own preconceptions or subconscious prejudices to his sources in order to elicit the conclusions he thinks he ought to reach.

---

[12] Hockett, *op. cit.*, pp. 59–79 and Johnson, *op. cit.*, pp. 50–75 contain adequate discussions of external criticism and cite salient examples.

[13] Not to be confused with internal analysis, a term employed for tests used in external criticism.

Nor should he be misled by figures of speech, hyperboles in disputations, or any peculiarities of style. The user of military records is fortunate, however, for good military documents are supposed to be written in exact, clear, sober language.

Once the author's meaning has been understood, it is necessary to determine the truth of his statements, for a document may be shown by external criticism to be a valid historical source and its meaning may be clear, yet it may be lacking in sincerity, accuracy, or both. For example, a biased, boastful personal memoir may be both insincere and inaccurate but still remain the best or only source of information on a given engagement. The task of the historian is to sift the truth from the errors, insincerities, deliberately false statements, and significant omissions. For example, estimates of enemy strength and dispositions are usually, from the nature of things, at once sincere but not accurate. In this instance, only access to enemy sources will serve to correct the errors. The erroneous estimates are in themselves historical facts, since these estimates served as part of the basis for judgment, decision, and action. In the same category are entries in journals regarding progress made during offensives. They usually are sincere, but where operations are being conducted over badly mapped or rough ground the distance covered is usually overestimated by the attacking unit. On the other hand, an insincere report may be perfectly accurate as far as it goes but may distort the truth by suppressing part of the facts.

There are several questions which the properly skeptical historian can put to his sources in the process of internal criticism:

Is the writer of a given document a good authority? Was he an eyewitness? If he was an eyewitness, can his testimony be relied on? Is he a trained observer? This necessary qualification is demonstrated by the story of the Wall Street explosion in 1920. Of nine eyewitnesses, eight testified that there were several vehicles of various kinds in the block where the explosion occurred and three of the eight were sure that a red motor truck carried the bomb. But the ninth eyewitness stated that the explosion took place on a small horse-drawn truck and that only one other vehicle, an automobile, was in sight. His testimony was subsequently proved to be correct.[14] If the eyewitnesses are good observers, theirs is the best, in fact the ultimate, testimony. Testimony of one reliable eyewitness is good, but the best evidence is the independent testimony of several eyewitnesses. But caution is needed here. Two eyewitnesses who tell exactly the same story have probably checked their stories and agreed on an official version. Honest, independent testimony from several eyewitnesses will normally contain several vari-

---

[14] Johnson, *op. cit.*, p. 24.

ations, variations which tend to indicate that the testimony is sincere and independent.

Was the writer biased? Here, of course, the writer of any after action or command report or any other account of an organization's activities is automatically subject to suspicion. Even if there is no conscious bias or deliberate attempt to falsify, a certain amount of unconscious bias will manifest itself in any number of ways—glossing over errors and failures; exaggerating the unit's successes and enemy casualties; listing all possible reasons for a failure, blaming other units ("Because the 18th Infantry on the right halted early in the afternoon, the 46th Infantry was forced to halt to protect its flank."); or failing to give credit to other units, services, or to allied forces. Commanders or participants reporting on their own activities can normally be expected to exaggerate, consciously or unconsciously, their own roles, and in dealing with quarrels, arguments, or disputes, to present their own points of view with more sympathy and understanding than those of opponents. Personal memoirs, even those based on diaries, are automatically suspect, for the temptations to justify oneself, to absolve oneself of blame, to claim credit, to get revenge for old scores, and to be wise after the event are all too strong.

Did the writer use reliable sources? The historian who publishes a book lists the sources of his information in footnotes, bibliography, or both, and these sources can and should be checked. Some military reports are not documented. An after action or command report is, however, submitted with supporting documents, such as orders, journals, and journal files, and can thus be checked against its sources. It should be noted that an after action or command report is technically a secondary account, not a primary source.

Under what circumstances was the narrative composed or the testimony given? This question is closely related to all the others, but a few sample questions may best illustrate it. Is the testimony given under oath? What is the purpose of the document? Why was it written? Does it analyze a problem or is it part of a body of documents dealing with a dispute? How long after the event was the narrative written or the testimony given? The best sources for opinions and beliefs, of course, are contemporary documents and statements.

Final Steps Before Writing

Now that the writer has chosen a subject, developed a bibliography, studied his material, organized his notes, and subjected his data to critical analysis, there are a few final steps to be taken before writing the draft. He should make a final check to make sure that no important sources have been overlooked. This can be accom-

390016 O - 56 - 6

plished by using the normal bibliographic aids and also by consulting recognized authorities in the field, if they are willing. He should also check through his material to make sure that there are no gaps in the story. If there are, more research is needed. Frequently the process of writing will itself show where there are gaps or omissions. Inadequate research, of course, almost always leads to errors.

The tentative outline should be rechecked and altered in accordance with the logic of the subject. This process will doubtless continue until the paper is complete.

The final step is of great importance. For it no exact rules can be stated; the student's own grasp of subject matter and logical methods must guide him. With virtually all the material collected organized, and evaluated, the student should analyze it carefully to determine its meaning and significance and to determine what new knowledge his paper will contribute. The meaning of the paper and its contribution constitute its theme. No matter how arduous the research that went into gathering material, the author must discard that which is not relevant to his subject. He must determine which aspects of his subject are to be emphasized and assign proportionate space in his paper accordingly. With this step, the processes of research have been practically completed. He is ready to write the section, chapter, or entire paper.

Writing the Draft

When To Write

Since methods of research vary with different writers, it is impossible to prescribe in advance the precise time to begin writing. This time will depend somewhat on the nature of the material and the plan by which the book is organized. For instance, Douglas S. Freeman treats the life of Washington in large segments, chronologically arranged, and completes one segment before beginning research on another. Not many projects, however, will lend themselves to this sort of treatment.

Writing cannot profitably begin until enough research has been completed to give the author a good general view of his subject, to afford a thorough sampling of various types of material, and to make sure that valid conclusions have been reached. Nor can the writing go very far until the data have been analyzed and the organization of the book has been planned. A book must be written, just as a house is built, according to a balanced, harmonious plan. This organization involves the sifting of relevant from irrelevant material, the selection and emphasis of important topics and ideas, and the determination of methods best suited for the treatment of the subject in hand. Certain subjects, for example, require a topical arrangement, certain others a chronological arrangement. Early care devoted to these matters will save much wasted effort as the work proceeds.

Nevertheless, most writers begin to write too late rather than too soon. It is a common failing to read, study, and search the material until it is "exhausted," before undertaking the work of composition. Though often due to a laudable desire for perfection this tendency is dangerous. It leads to undue accumulation of notes until the writer is so overwhelmed in a mass of detail that he loses sight of "the big picture." Some writers have devoted their lives to taking notes without ever writing.

For economy of effort, writing should begin before research is complete. Nothing else reveals so clearly those areas where research is ample and those where further investigation is needed. The gaps may be passed over and filled in later. Many authors find it practicable to begin writing at a point where their research is about half-way complete—but no final rule can be applied to every project. One experienced historian says that he begins to write when he is first able to "see" his subject, that is, when its main outlines take definite form in his mind. For flexibility in adding, deleting, and rearranging material, loose-leaf form should be used.

Writing Aids

The writer of books will accumulate all the physical equipment needed before he starts the actual work of writing. Such equipment, if possible, should be immediately available where the writer works, not stored in some distant place. The following items will be constantly needed by the military historian:

Maps. Since military operations are planned and executed with the aid of maps, no profitable study of these operations is possible without the same aid. Maps are scarce and inaccurate during the early history of the United States, a fact which affected adversely both military campaigns and military history. In recent years maps have been greatly improved. For operations covering a large area, a good globe is often helpful.

Photographs. If available, aerial photographs, both oblique and vertical, are invaluable supplements to maps. Details of equipment and terrain are also frequently recorded in photographs. In the case of both maps and photographs, the author should avail himself especially of those that were used or taken in connection with the events which he is recording.

Historical and Geographical Atlases. Such works are particularly helpful when they supply facts of a social, economic, or political nature for the period under consideration.

Chronologies.   Reliable chronologies, whether published or in documentary form, are of the highest value.   If none are available for the period in question, the writer will do well to make his own chronology from his source material.   Such care will be of great help in avoiding errors.

Military Reference Works.   These works include field service regulations, field manuals, technical manuals, tables of organization and equipment, official registers of Army, Navy, and Air Force officers, and many other items—all of which can be secured for any recent period.   It goes without saying that every writer's study should also contain copies of general reference works such as good dictionaries and encyclopedias.

Qualities of Good Writing

When Anatole France, one of the great stylists of his age, was asked for the secret of his art he replied, "First clarity, second clarity, and finally clarity."   So important is this quality that its full attainment results almost automatically in unity, coherence, force, emphasis, and the various other qualities traditionally enunciated by rhetoricians.   Recognition of the principle, however, is only the first step toward its practice.

Practice of Good Writing

Like every other art, writing cannot be taught by rule or precept. Strictly speaking, it cannot be taught at all—each writer must learn for himself.   The following suggestions are offered as an encouragement to learn:

Attitude Toward Writing.   The actual writing of a book should be considered not a burden but a challenge.   Unfortunately some scholars regard writing as merely a painful necessity, an unwelcome adjunct to their research.   In reality it is one of the greatest of the arts, mastery of which should be a cause for pride.   American scholarship is second to none for its thoroughness and objectivity, yet most scholarly writing in this country is dull and flat, comparing unfavorably in its form and presentation with the work of foreign scholars.   The reason is not hard to find.   Only the exceptional American scholar has been thoroughly grounded in the great classics of English literature or has much regard for writing as an art.   In their passion for specialization many scholars are impatient of writing as such, somewhat scornfully relegating to poets and journalists any concern for the art of expression.   So long as this attitude persists, few American historians will write like Toynbee, few biologists like Julian Huxley.   Such notable exceptions as Carl Becker and Charles Beard in history, Ruth Benedict in anthropology, merely emphasize the point.

Learn To Write by Reading.   Nothing can be done without a standard—and the standard for writers is found in the work of great writers.   These standards are fundamentally the same for all kinds of writing and they are no less important for works of scientific or historical scholarship than for novels and plays.   Reading with alertness and discernment, the ambitious writer will be aware of form as well as content and thus, by analysis and induction, understand why certain writing is good and other writing bad.   When he finds, for instance, that Bertrand Russell can express highly intricate ideas in the most simple and lucid prose, he will no longer be content with ambiguous statements, jargon-like terminology, or a sentence structure so involved as to require two readings.

Unity and Coherence.   Unity demands a singleness of effect, a completeness and wholeness without excess in one part or lack in another.   It implies a right proportion for everything.   Unity is attained for the book as a whole by careful planning.   It is attained for sentences, paragraphs, and chapters by presenting one idea at a time.   If chapter X reechoes and overlaps material in chapter II, unity has been violated.   Coherence is the principle by which parts of the book are held together, a principle based on logical development.   Each paragraph, each chapter, should build on what has gone before.   Coherence requires not only an orderly arrangement but a proper linking of part to part by means of transitional material wherever needed.   The author should not assume that his reader can supply such transitions for himself.

Emphasis.   Emphasis is a matter of both content and form.   It involves, first, a sure judgment as to the relative importance of various materials and of ideas based on those materials.   The relation of one fact to another must be carefully considered.   Second, emphasis involves presenting the material in as forceful a way as possible.   This is partly a matter of style, partly of arrangement. Building up to a conclusion, to a sense of climax, is important for historical writing as well as fiction.

Sentence Structure.   The first requirement of sentence structure is that it should be immediately clear, with no possibility of misinterpretation or ambiguity.   The author should strive for simplicity, straightforwardness, conciseness.   Particular attention should be paid to the reference of pronouns; avoid using *it, this,* or *they* without a definite antecedent.

Once clearness is assured, some attention should be paid to variety.   If all the sentences are short the effect will be choppy; if they are all long, the reader's attention will tire.   Nor should every sentence begin with the main clause.   Monotony can be avoided by drawing on the rich store of subordinating words found in the English language, such words as *since, although, because, before, after, where, when,* and *while.* Subordinate clauses introduced by these words may be placed either before or after the main clause.

Diction. Selecting exactly the right word to express a particular meaning is one of the writer's hardest tasks. This task will be greatly lightened if the author has a lifelong familiarity with strong and simple idiom and direct, concrete expression as well as with more abstract expression. Words have not merely a literal meaning—*denotation*—but a flavor, an associational value—*connotation.* For example, a writer may state either that a thing is "hard to do" or that it is "difficult to accomplish." The denotation of the two expressions is almost identical, the connotation is quite different. Thus the relative force, dignity, formality, or informality of a term is fully as important as its literal meaning. The linguistic "level" on which a book is written will depend partly on the subject matter, partly on the author's stylistic preference. Even in scholarly writing, a formal style of the 19th century is being replaced by more simple and direct expression.

Technical Terms and Jargon. Every branch of learning has its legitimate technical terms, words needed to express concepts that can be expressed in no other way. Examples of such terms in military history are *angle of approach, collimation, critical item, troop basis.* When technical terms are used unnecessarily, or to conceal rather than convey meaning, they become jargon. Doctors and lawyers use jargon to conceal facts; pedants use it to parade their learning. A proper use of technical terms is indispensable, but excessive use of jargon is not only bad style but often indicates a lack of clear thinking.

Trite Expressions. Many words and phrases have been over-used until they have lost their freshness and hence have no clear-cut meaning. Often they had no clear meaning to begin with and came into vogue among writers and speakers who had no clear thought to express. Note, for instance, the flat indefiniteness of such words as *worthwhile* and *outstanding.* A careful writer will select a more exact word such as *excellent, notable, prominent, chief, conspicuous, illustrious, celebrated.* Only wide reading and long practice can give a sure touch in this sort of thing—but every good handbook of English contains a list of trite expressions to be avoided.

Authentic Background of the Period Studied

It is a common failing of novelists and playwrights to depict a past period in terms of their own, not merely in external details but in fundamental ideas. For example, the writings of Shakespeare are full of anachronisms—a clock strikes in Julius Caesar's time, pistols are carried by soldiers of the 13th century, and ancient rulers express the ideals of British chivalry. Such departures from fact are perhaps not very important for poetic drama, which seeks rather to be true to human nature. They are highly important for historians, but not all historians succeed in avoiding them.

The serious student of history must make himself thoroughly familiar with the background of the period in which his work lies. The military historian must know what weapons, communications, supply facilities, maps, roads, bridges, and vehicles were available to the commanders who planned the strategy and tactics of any war in the past to which the historian turns his attention. A present-day map will be of little value in studying Grant's campaigns around Richmond; only a map of the period will show what roads and other physical features existed at the time.

The life of the common soldier, his feelings and attitudes, are no less important. What food did he eat, what clothes did he wear, what shelter did he have? What care, if any, was taken for his health? At just what time did anaesthesia and aseptic surgery show their effect on battle casualties? What conditions affected the soldier's morale? What news of the war did he receive, what mail from home? What political and cultural ideas dominated those who were fighting to defend them?

In answering these questions the historian must take advantage of every resource available—official records, diaries, letters, autobiographies, photographs, sketches of military artists, and contemporary newspapers. From these sources he should bring his narrative to life, enabling the reader to picture the terrain and the weather, understand the people who lived in the area, appreciate the personality, the genius, the limitations of the high commanders, and follow the sights and sounds of the battle as if he were there.

Depth of Research

The author should probe deep for the causes of success and failure of the national military effort and of the armed forces in the field. This will necessitate a critical and definitive examination of source material bearing on the topic or subject being studied. The task is more difficult in victory than in defeat. At the highest level it should include an examination of the national potentials for war; of national objectives; of the higher organization for war; and of the relations of military policy to foreign and domestic policy and the degree of balance and coordination existing among these factors; and interallied coordination at the national level. At lower operational levels it should include an examination of interallied coordination; coordination of the sea, ground, and air elements; organization; logistics; armament; tactics; training; and the actual combat in which American forces are pitted against those of the enemy.

Openmindedness and Objectivity

A historian must be openminded toward his material at all times. Laying aside all conscious prejudice he must ascertain the facts through critical examination of all available records. Having done this he is in a position to relate one set of facts to another and draw conclusions based on the evidence uncovered. The wider his knowledge, the more thorough his research; and the more objective his approach, the sounder his conclusions will be. The following instructions given to historical officers in a World War II directive are generally applicable to the writing of all military history:

> Attention will be concentrated on major policies, problems, and accomplishments of the command together with the lessons learned.
>
> The history should state not only *what* was done but *how* and *why* it was done.
>
> . . . The history must include a candid and factual account of difficulties, mistakes recognized as such, the means by which, in the opinion of those concerned, they might have been avoided, the measures used to overcome them, and the effectiveness of such measures. The history will not serve the purpose if purely laudatory.

Historical Writing of Current Military Events

A military historian of current events is frequently only doing basic research for a future historian. He should, therefore, try to anticipate requirements of the future historian. This means that he must secure information that answers the questions: "What was done?" "How was it done?" "Why was it done?"

The success of a military historian *in writing on current activities* will depend greatly upon the degree to which he measures up to the ideals and mental requirements of a sound historian. In no field of historical writing is there greater demand for objectivity, intellectual honesty, and sound judgment. In addition he needs determination, tact, a sense of discretion, and other qualities that are necessary to get at the facts on which sound history can be based. He must avoid being a flatterer or a nuisance, a sycophant, or a carping critic. He must constantly be on guard against the danger of becoming an apologist, a propagandist, or a mudslinger.

The historian of current events doubtless will have to fight many a battle within himself in order to maintain strict objectivity toward friend and foe alike. Only by so doing, however, can either the immediate or permanent interests of his country be properly served. It is not expected that he remain neutral, for as often as not the record will show a preponderance of evidence on one side or the other of an issue or controversy. Only when diligent research brings to light fragmentary or contradictory evidence should the historian refrain from drawing conclusions. In such cases, however, he should define the point at issue precisely and point out why no judgment can be made at the time. By so doing he will justify his own work and indicate the area in which research is needed as more evidence becomes available.

The historian of current events should remember, in his writing as in his research, to ask himself whether the text will be adequate to a future reader who may have no other source of information to guide him. In his writing he should, therefore, use simple, direct language, taking special pains to avoid any chance of being misunderstood. It is far better to repeat names, places, and the like, than to risk confusion in an effort to achieve an interesting or varied style. The historian's vocabulary should aim at general intelligibility. Military terms should be used, but always in their normally accepted meanings. Special terminology or modifications of general vocabulary peculiar to a unit, theater, or country should be clearly explained.

Use of Assembled Data in Writing Draft

Many first drafts are poorly written because the author is too much a slave to his note-slips. By following his notes too closely he loses the clearness, coherence, and "flow" that finished work should have. An experienced teacher of graduate students has suggested that the writer select a block of notes which forms the basis for a chapter and assimilate it by repeated reading. The notes are then laid aside and the chapter written "with an easy elbow." Such a practice helps in avoiding too much petty detail and excessive quotation. For the final draft the notes are again consulted for greater accuracy, the insertion of quotations, and the preparation of footnotes.

Perfecting the Draft

The process of perfecting a draft manuscript will vary with each author. It will be determined in great part by the depth of the author's initial research and his attention to details of both content and style. The suggestions which follow may be adopted and varied to fit the requirements of each individual project.

When an author is doing his research and writing his first draft, he should compile a list of participants and authorities who have knowledge of the subject with which he is working. After each draft chapter is finished it should be reviewed by the author's supervisor or by a personal advisor. Once the first draft is completed, the author should revise and polish his manuscript incorporating the suggestions of the supervisor or advisor. The manuscript should then receive its preliminary editing and be reproduced in a sufficient number of copies for all review purposes.

The author should select from the list of those having special knowledge of his subject the names of individuals who may be able to make valuable comments and suggestions. The covering letters sent out with copies of the manuscript should be very carefully prepared; if a reviewer has special knowledge of one phase of the study he should be requested to comment particularly on that phase. Sometimes individuals who give little information in response to questionnaires or in interviews will comment extensively on a manuscript. The reviewer approaches a manuscript with a fresh point of view and is likely to see inaccuracies and omissions overlooked by someone who has worked more closely with it.

Comments and suggestions received from reviewers should be compared and evaluated. One way of doing this is to enter the comments in a copy of the draft manuscript. Whatever additional research is necessary to correct errors of fact and clarify the manuscript should then be completed. After the author has inserted all additions and changes in a master copy of the draft, he should complete his final revision of the entire manuscript which should then be reviewed again by the author's supervisor before it receives its final editing.

Documentation

Full and accurate documentation is the stamp of authenticity which the scholar places on his work. By this means he frankly reveals to the reader the sources of his information. The character of these sources will do much to establish the author's skill—or his lack of it—in the evaluation of evidence. The documentation will also reveal to what extent the author has made use of the sources available in his field and to what extent he has been able to discover sources not previously known.

Each fact stated, unless a matter of common knowledge or one which can readily be verified elsewhere, should be accurately documented in the footnotes. Since the documentation is designed to aid scholars in further study of the subject, full information should be given about the documents. The following facts should be included, in the order given: nature of the document (letter, memorandum, report); the originator; the recipient; the date; the subject, if given; the file designation; and the file location. Each footnote should immediately follow the line of text containing the reference number applying to that note; a line should be drawn or typed (use the same character as for underlining) above and below the footnote to separate it from the text. This method is preferred by printers. For brevity, all standard abbreviations may be used. At times the nature of the material is such that space can be saved and the number of footnotes reduced by consolidating all references for a paragraph in one note with several items.

Footnotes should not be too heavily loaded with discursive or explanatory material. Generally such material, if worth using at all, can be more effectively included in the main text. Though many Latin terms, or their abbreviations, are commonly used in footnotes, there is a growing tendency to avoid their use. For example, "above" and "below" are replacing *supra* and *infra*. *Ibid.* (*ibidem*, in the same place) should be used to refer only to material in an immediately preceding note. For a full discussion of footnote form, see section III, appendix A.

Bibliography

Sources should be grouped according to type, and each major group of records briefly described. The physical location of the files at the time consulted should be indicated. Published works should be grouped separately and listed by author, title, place and date of publication, and name of publisher.

Tables, Charts, Maps, Illustrations

Each table or chart, except those that are very short and informal, should have a number and a title. Dates should also be included in the title. Maps should be numbered, titled, and dated. Those which show the action of military units should employ the "Basic Military Map Symbols." Photographs should be closely tied in with the text, and none should be used which do not definitely clarify matter in the text. The sources of all tables, charts, maps, and illustrations should be clearly indicated.

APPENDIX A
STYLE MANUAL

Section I.   INTRODUCTION

This appendix is designed to cover points of usage not covered in official style manuals that are of special concern to historians.   It should be used in conjunction with the 1953 edition of the Government Printing Office *Style Manual.*   Where the GPO *Style Manual* or *Webster's New International Dictionary* differ from Army dictionaries in matters of spelling or capitalization, the Army form is to be followed.[1]

Section II.   USAGE

Capitalization

For capitalization of technical military terms not found in ordinary usage follow SR 320–5–1, "Dictionary of United States Army Terms."

Military Terms

Capitalize terms which, though consisting of common adjectives, have a special meaning in military usage.

> Blue armies (maneuvers)

Type Allied code names in solid caps.

> Operation TORCH   OMAHA Beach

Type enemy code names in solid caps and italicize.

> Operation *SEELOEWE*

Titles of Publications and Their Parts

Capitalize but do not italicize:
> Army Regulations
> Mobilization Regulations
> War Department General Mobilization Plan

Preferred Spellings

Refer to Webster's *New International Dictionary.*   For military words consult SR 320–5–1.

---

[1] APPENDIX A, *Style Manual,* has been developed in the Office of the Chief of Military History and has proved its value both as an aid to historians and to the Editorial Section.

Follow British spelling in British designations.

Refer to the lists of the U. S. Board on Geographic Names for spelling of place names. See also section on "Foreign Geographic Terms," below.

Abbreviations and Symbols

Abbreviate in the text only elements which have become established in ordinary usage, in military usage, or occur frequently. For abbreviations in footnotes, charts, and tables see the sections under those headings.

Write abbreviations in solid caps in parentheses after the complete term the first time it is used in any volume. Subsequent uses require only the abbreviation. Do not use periods after abbreviations in solid caps.

Do not abbreviate in titles or headings.

Military and Naval Abbreviations (See SR 320–50–1)

Do not abbreviate common nouns standing for military units, except in tables, charts, lists, and footnotes.

Company A   32d Infantry

Abbreviate designations of rank and grade if the full name is written out. (For exceptions see "Military Rank and Titles," below.)

Capt. Alexander R. Skinker   *but* Captain Skinker

S. Sgt. Herbert H. Burr   Sergeant Burr

In certain compound abbreviations consisting of two capital letters the letters are separated by the sign /.

T/O (Table of Organization)   *but* ZI

T/E (Table of Equipment)

Do not use punctuation after an abbreviation when used with a figure giving a weapon's caliber.

155-mm howitzer   *but* 10.3 mm. long

Indicate British nationality of naval craft by *H. M. S.*

H. M. S. *Hood*   or the British battle cruiser *Hood*

Italics

Italicize

Foreign words and phrases.

Names of specific enemy military units.

Do not Italicize

Titles of manuals, circulars, and bulletins which are not published for general distribution. Capitalize initial letters of important words and place in quotes.

Quotations

Type all quoted material exactly as in the original.

Run into the text, with quotation marks, quotations of fewer than seven typed lines.   Separate and single-space quotations of seven typed lines or more.

Place the footnote reference mark at the end of the quotation whether run-in or separated.

Indicate omissions within quotations by ellipses (three periods) in addition to necessary punctuation marks such as the period at the end of the sentence.   If the omission occurs after the end of a sentence, place the first period close to the last letter; if the omission occurs just before the end of a sentence, separate the last period from the ellipses by a space; if the omission occurs in the middle of a sentence, leave a space before and after the periods.

Separated quotations

Single-space and indent five spaces.

Do not use quotation marks with separated quotations except to indicate a quotation within the quotation.

Indent the first line of a separated quotation unless the first line begins in the middle of a sentence.   If a separated quotation begins in the middle of a sentence, use ellipses and do not indent.

Do not introduce a separated quotation by *that,* except when the first sentence of the quoted material is incomplete and requires it. Use terms such as *as follows, wrote, declared, reported,* followed by a colon.

Dates and Time

Dates

Use military dating in text and all footnotes except in quotation or in citing titles of documents in which a different system is used.

    31 July 1946   *but* Act of July 6, 1942
    July 1946

Abbreviate months and years only in tables, charts, and footnotes. Use military abbreviations (first three letters of month).

    29 Jun 46   *not* 29 June '46   *or* 29 Sep 1946

Time

Indicate time in connection with military activity according to military practice, on the 24-hour basis.   It is not necessary to add the letter indicating the time zone or the word *hours.*

    Action started at 0845.

Indicate time not referring to military activity in the ordinary manner.

Congress recessed at 11 P.M.

Do not use *at about* to indicate an approximate designation of time. *About* is sufficient: *about 0600.*

Avoid tautology such as *0600 in the morning.*

Use the military abbreviations *D-day, H-hour, V-E Day,* and *V-J Day.*

In connection with D-day, do not write days after the numeral; with H-hour, do not write hours after the numeral.

   D+4   H−4

Any other time element is shown in parentheses.

   D+4 (months)   H−4 (minutes)

Military Organizations

Short names of military organizations may be used.

   the Air Force   the Field Forces

If names of organizations have changed, use the name which prevailed at the time.

   War Department (before 15 Sep 47)   Department of the Army

If there is a possibility of confusion, identify the unit by nationality, especially in the first mention.

Do not begin a sentence with the numeral or letter of a unit.

Infantry may be omitted in the designation of American infantry divisions.   Indicate other branches of the service.

   1st Division   1st Armored Division

Regiment may be omitted in the designation of a single American infantry regiment.

   26th Infantry   *but* the 16th and 18th Infantry Regiments

Write out numbers of U. S. armies.

   Third Army   Eighth Army

Use Roman numerals for U. S. corps.

   I Corps   II Corps

Use arabic numerals for divisions, regiments, battalions, platoons, and squads.

   1st Squad, 2d Platoon
   2d Battalion, 327th Glider Infantry, 101st Airborne Division

Designations of U. S. Navy and Marine Corps Units

U. S. Navy

Third Fleet	Carrier Division 1
VII Amphibious Force	Fighting Squadron 22 (VF 22)
Task Force 31	3d Construction Battalion
Task Group 61.1	

U. S. Marine Corps

I Marine Amphibious Corps   2d Battalion, 12th Marines
4th Marine Division   1st Marine Air Wing
6th Marines   Marine Air Group 23
Marine Fighting Squadron 233 (VMF 233)
Marine Scout Bombing Squadron (VMSB 232)

Foreign Military Units

Italicize specific enemy units.

Translate all foreign terms which parallel the English version; otherwise, use the foreign terms.

Retain special distinguishing names or honorifics with a unit's number.

Honorable 3d Division

National Unit Designations

British

21 Army Group   the South Staffordshire Regi-
First Army   ment or S. Staffords
3 Corps   1st Battalion, North Stafford-
1st Division   shire Regiment, or 1 N. Staffs
1st Brigade

Australia

First Army   2/22 Battalion
I Corps   No. 5 (Maintenance) Group
7th Division   No. 82 (Bomber) Wing
8th Brigade   No. 76 (Transport) Wing
New South Wales Regiment   No. 30 (Interceptor-Fighter)
45th Field Regiment   Squadron

New Zealand

3d Division   No. 42 Transport Squadron
8th Brigade   No. 43 Fighter Squadron
1st Battalion   No. 41 Bomber-Reconnaissance
   Squadron

French

1st Army   4th Infantry Brigade
1st Corps   8th Moroccan Infantry
1st Motorized Division   1st Battalion, 8th Moroccan In-
3d Algerian Infantry Divi-   fantry
     sion

Chinese

IX War Area	36th Division
XX Group Army	Honorable 2d Division
XVIII Route Army	4th (Cavalry) Brigade
	259th Infantry
	1st Battalion, 259th Infantry

Italian (italicized when enemy unit)

Army Group Central Italy	205th Coastal Division
First Army	6th Aosta Infantry Regiment
XXI Corps	14th Murge Artillery Regiment
6th Cuneo Division	7th Mortar Battalion
2d Sforzesca (semi-motor- ized) Division	1st Battalion, 6th Aosta Infantry

German

Army Group B	*1st Brigade*
First Army	*1st Regiment*
I Corps	*1st Battalion*
1st Division	

Japanese

Southern Area Army	*3d Division*
1st Area Army	*4th Brigade*
2d Army	*228th Infantry*
	1st Battalion, 228th Infantry

Russian

First Ukrainian Front	19th Infantry Division
Seventh Guard Army	30th Antitank Brigade
XX Armored Corps	105th Guard Regiment
	6th Signal Battalion

Military Rank and Titles

Initial Mention

In the initial reference to an individual give full rank (abbr.), full name (first name, middle initial, and surname).

Lt. Col. John C. Black	Rear Adm. Daniel J. Callaghan
Pfc. Floyd K. Lindstrom	S. Sgt. Walter D. Ehlers
Pvt. Ova A. Kelley	Cpl. John Kinsey

390016 O - 56 - 7

Subsequent Mentions

Colonel Black	Admiral Callaghan
Private Lindstrom	Sergeant Ehlers
Private Kelley	Corporal Kinsey

Do not in any case abbreviate the following titles in the text:

General of the Army	Fleet Admiral
Chief of Staff	

Foreign Military Rank and Titles

At first mention, write the full name of general and flag officers, including honorifics and rank, in the foreign term, not italicized. Thereafter use the English language equivalent for rank and only the last name.

General der Panzertruppen Hermann Balck, General Balck
Brigadier Sir Godfrey Rhodes, Brigadier Rhodes
Admiral Sir Bertram Ramsay, Admiral Ramsay

Below the rank of general and flag officers, use the English equivalent. As in the case of rank in the U. S. Army, abbreviate at first mention.

Foreign Words

Italicize foreign words and phrases which have not been anglicized. In each case, refer to *Webster's International Dictionary*, especially the Addenda.

Do not italicize foreign titles preceding proper names.

Reichmarschall Goering   Pere Lagrange
Freiherr von Schenau

Do not italicize names of foreign organizations or institutions (except enemy military units).

The Alliance Francaise	the Reichstag
Organization Todt	the Bibliotheque Nationals

Do not italicize the following Latin terms:

cf.	e.g.	viz
i.e.	etc.	vs.

Do not italicize generic references to enemy military units.

a panzer grenadier division

Retain foreign diacritical marks except the German umlaut; to indicate the umlaut, use the letter *e* after the *a, o,* or *u.*

Saarbruecken

Foreign Geographic Terms

Do not italicize foreign geographic names.

Refer to the lists of the U. S. Board on Geographic Names for form and spelling.

Translate foreign common nouns such as *river, peninsula,* and *bay,* in names of well-known geographic features.

Bay of the Seine   *but* Cap de la Hague

Translate proper nouns in foreign geographic terms if an English equivalent has become well established.

Florence   *but* Chantilly
Rome   Rouen

If a place is not named on an official map but received a name as a result of military operation, the practice is to use the given name, where this appears in the military records of the operations, followed or footnoted by military coordinates and a reference to the map used. If the available maps are not gridded, use latitude and longitude.

Section III. FOOTNOTES

Style

In the early draft and the final copy sent to the editor, the footnotes should *not* be numbered but rather an asterisk placed where the reference number will appear. This eliminates any confusion that might result in the shifting of paragraphs or pages by the editor. After the editing has been completed and reviewed by the author, the footnotes are numbered consecutively within each chapter.

In the early drafts, footnotes should be double-spaced for the convenience of the editor. In the copy sent to the printer, footnotes should be single-spaced.

Type the reference number and footnote thus:

revised its estimates for 1947.* (^{21})   Later in the

---

* (^{21})
Memo, OPD for Budget Officer, 16 Feb 45, sub: Strength of the Army.   WDCSA 320.2 (1946) Case 55.   DRB, TAG.

(*Note.* Type reference number superior, in text and footnote.
Type full lines above and below footnote to separate from text.
Indent first line of footnote to paragraph indention.)

Footnote reference number for a run-in table should be in the box head. If no box head, number should come at the end of preceding text.

Footnote reference number for a direct quotation should follow the quotation, not the preceding text.

Abbreviation and Capitalization

Abbreviate and capitalize as in text, and also according to the abbreviations section of *Webster's International Dictionary* and SR 320–50–1. *No periods are required in military usage.*

Abbreviate and capitalize:

After *sub* (capitalize important words).   Do not abbreviate titles of official circulars, orders, reports, or the like.

Parts of publications and documents:

art.	par.	*but* Item
bk.	pt.	No.
ch.	sec.	
n.	ser.	
p.	vol.	

Documents:

Bul	(Bulletin)	Memo	(Memorandum)
Cir	(Circular)	MC	(Message Center)
CM	(Classified Message)	Min	(Minutes)
Conf	(Conference)	Ms	(Manuscript)
Corr	(Correspondence)	Msg	(Message)
EO	(Executive Order)	Mtg	(Meeting)
FO	(Field Order)	PL	(Public Law)
GO	(General Order)	Rad	(Radiogram)
Incl	(Inclosure)	Rpt	(Report)
Ind	(Indorsement)	SO	(Special Order)
Interv	(Interview)	Teleg	(Telegram)
Ltr	(Letter)	Sitrep	(Situation Report)

File locations:

Bx	(Box)	*but* Binder
Bdl	(Bundle)	Cabinet
Env	(Envelope)	Case
Exec	(Executive)	Drawer
Rm	(Room)	Folder
Sec	(Section)	Item
Ser	(Serial)	

Commands:

CINCPAC   USAFFE

Do not abbreviate titles of documents.

Do not abbreviate: *but* Adm
  General of the Army   Gen
  President (of the   CofS
    United States)
  Fleet Admiral

Use the abbreviation *No.* only to avoid ambiguity.

Format

Commercial Publications

Books

Author, first name first, comma
Full title, italicized,
Place, comma, year of publication, in parentheses, comma
Volume and page references, period.
[Do not write *vol.* except to avoid ambiguity.]
Volume numbers are given in upper case Roman, pages in
 Arabic.
Examples in first reference to books:
One author:
 Robert E. Sherwood, *Roosevelt and Hopkins: An Intimate History*
  (New York, 1948), p. 627.
Two authors:
 Charles G. Haines and Ross J. Hoffman, *Origins and Back-
  ground of the Second World War* (London and New York,
  1943), p. 89.
Three authors:
 List names of all as with two authors.
More than three authors:
 List the complete name of the first author followed by "and
  Others."
No author:
 Dragoon Campaigns to the Rocky Mountains (New York, 1836),
  p. 174.
A later edition:
 A Manual of Style (11th ed.; Chicago, 1949), p. 140.
An edited work:
 The Poems of Edgar Allan Poe, ed. Killis Campbell (Boston,
  1917), p. 42.
A translated work:
 Carl von Clausewitz, *On War,* trans. J. J. Graham (London,
  1918), I, p. 77.
Joint project:
 Kentucky, Federal Writers Project, *Military History of Ken-
  tucky* (Frankfort, 1939), pp. 79–96.
A book in a series:
 Military Obligation: The American Tradition ("Backgrounds of
  Selective Service," Monograph No. I, vol. II, pt. II [Wash-
  ington, 1947]), p. 3.
Subsequent references when not immediately following:

Sherwood, *op. cit.,* p. 444.

A Manual of Style, op. cit., p. 167.

Clausewitz, *op. cit.,* I, p. 89.

Kentucky, Federal Writers Project, *op. cit.,* p. 286.

When two books by the same author are cited, *op. cit.* cannot be used.

John McAuley Palmer, *America in Arms* (New Haven, 1941), pp. 6–13.

John McAuley Palmer, *Washington-Lincoln-Wilson, Three War Statesmen* (New York, 1930), pp. 325, 372, 380.

Palmer, *America in Arms,* p. 19.

Palmer, *Washington-Lincoln-Wilson,* p. 329.

Where references to the same work follow each other consecutively and uninterruptedly, use *ibid.* instead of repeating the title.

Robert E. Sherwood, *Roosevelt and Hopkins: An Intimate History* (New York, 1938), p. 627.

Ibid., p. 572.

John McAuley Palmer, *America in Arms* (New Haven, 1941), pp. 6–13.

Ibid., p. 74.

Periodicals

Author, first name first, comma

Article, title, in quotes, comma

Periodical title, italicized, comma

Volume, year (in parentheses), comma

Page reference, period

Franklin L. Ford, "The Twentieth of July in the History of German Resistance," *American Historical Review,* LI (July 1945), pp. 609–26.

When using *ibid.* for references to periodicals, repeat the volume number.

Op. cit. may be used in reference to periodicals if the name of the author and article are repeated.

Ford, "The Twentieth of July in the History of German Resistance," *op. cit.,* p. 614.

or

Ford, *American Historical Review,* LI (1945), p. 614.

Newspapers

Give the place of publication, the name of the newspaper, the date, and page number. Italicize the name of the newspaper, and the place of publication if it is a part of the name. *The* is not italicized even though part of the name.

The *New York Times,* 14 Aug 45, p. 8.

When the place of publication is not given, add it in brackets to avoid ambiguity, as:

The [Baltimore] *Sun,* 25 Aug 45, p. 20.

The [Washington] *Evening Star,* 21 Dec 45.

Archival Material

Before citing any material in the National Archives, the author should consult with an archivist to ascertain proper record group, series, etc.

Use commas within an element in a citation; periods to separate elements; and semicolons to separate a series of citations.

Use a colon after *sub.*

Form:

Character of the document, comma

Writer and/or issuing agency, to/for

Recipient (individual or agency), comma

Date, comma

Subject or title, period.

File designation (detailed exactly as on file), period.

Location of file, period.

[100] Memo, Tompkins to DCofS, 5 Jan 44, sub: Schedule. WDSPD 380 (12 Aug 43).   DRB, TAG.

[119] Memo, Tompkins for Marshall, 8 Feb 44, sub: Troop Bases.   OPD 370.9, Case 12.   DRB, TAG; DF, SPD to OPD, 7 Mar 44, sub: Troop Bases.   SPD Study 33, sec. II.   DRB, TAG.

[8] Memo, AWC Bd to SW, 17 Mar 03, sub: Equipment and Organization of Military Forces.   Records of WDGS, 3d Div. National Archives.

[*Note.*   For National Archives files do not use record group number, but either full name or abbreviation of issuing office.]

[50] Memo, CofWCD to CofS, 3 Feb 17, sub: Preparations for possible hostilities with Germany.   WCD Files 9433/4. Copy filed as incl to memo, Lt. G. E. Adamson (aide to Pershing) to TAG, 20 Feb 23, sub: Request for information on prewar plans.   AG File 381.   National Archives.

[53] Statement, Brig Gen O. F. Lange (Ret).   HIS 330.14. OCMH

[72] Interview, Brig Gen O. F. Lange (Ret), 4 Feb 49.   Author's file.

Ibid. may be used in citing archival material when references to the same work follow each other uninterruptedly.   *Op. cit.* is never used in connection with archival material.

The classification of a document or file (C), (S), or (TS), directly follows the title of the document or the file number as:

Ltr, Hq ASF to DCofS for Svc Cmds, 13 Mar 44, sub: Italian Service Units (C). ASF 383.6 Italian Service Units (S). DRB, TAG.

Unpublished Manuscripts

[62] Lecture, Dr. George H. Gallup, American Institute of Public Opinions, before the Industrial College of the Armed Forces, 17 Jun 47. L47-150. Industrial College Library.

[172] Col L. W. Cass, "History of the First Replacement Depot, AEF," 27 Feb 19. [No file number.] MS in NWC Library.

[107] Rpt, Com No. 5, AWC, 31 Oct 34, sub: Replacements. 1-1935-5, p. 13. NWC Library.

Both *ibid.* and *op. cit.* may be used in citing unpublished material, as:

Gallup, lecture, *op. cit.*
Cass, *op. cit.*
Report of Committee No. 5, AWC, *op. cit.*

Government Publications

In citing Government publications it is not necessary to list place of publication; date of publication is given only to avoid ambiguity. Italicize date if part of the title:

"Report of The Adjutant General," *War Department Annual Reports, 1920,* I, p. 47.

Annual Report of the Secretary of War, 1924, p. 43.

Biennial Report of the Chief of Staff of the United States Army, July 1, 1941 to June 30, 1943 . . . , p. 25.

The name of the signator of the official report or document may be cited if the author feels it is of sufficient importance or significance.

In citing general orders, bulletins, etc., do not write No. before the numeral.

WD GO 37, 10 Aug 42.
DA Bul 10, 19 Sep 51.

Titles of Army studies, manuals, etc. that have not been published for general distribution or have been mimeographed are placed in quotation marks.

TM 30-944, "Dictionary of Spoken Russian".

Maj J. C. Sparrow, "History of Personnel Demobilization in the United States Army" (Special Studies Series, OCMH), 1951.

DA Pam 20-210, *History of Personnel Demobilization in the United States Army,* Jul 52.

H. R. Rpt. 1667, 78th Cong., 2d sess., "Legislative Appropriation Bill, 1939," 18 Jun 44.

S. Doc. 79, 78th Cong., 2d sess., "Agriculture Appropriation Bill, 1939," 4 Apr 44.

Hearings before a Subcommittee of the Committee on Appropriations, U. S. Senate, 78th Cong., 2d sess. on H.R. 9621, H.R. 9622, H.R. 9623, H.R. 9624, H.R. 9625, H.R. 7685, 1944.
[If title of bill is given in place of S. or H.R. number, place the title in quotes.]

PL 299, 78th Cong., 2d sess., 30 Sep 44.

Act of April 22, 1898.   30 *Stat.* 361
[If possible give general order or bulletin and date in which the law was reprinted.]

Official Histories

Robert R. Palmer, Bell I. Wiley, and William R. Keast, *The Procurement and Training of Ground Combat Troops* in UNITED STATES ARMY IN WORLD WAR II (Washington, 1948), pp. 165–239.

Reports of Commander-in-Chief, A.E.F., Staff Sections and Services in UNITED STATES ARMY IN THE WORLD WAR, 1917–1919 (Washington, 1948), XIV, pp. 33–38.

Section IV.   FORMAT

Front Matter

General

The front matter in a comprehensive military history is arranged as follows: title page, copyright page, dedication, foreword, preface, table of contents, lists of tables, charts, maps, and illustrations.

Pages should be numbered so that the odd numbers are always on the right-hand side, and the even on the left.   Each new chapter, the preface, foreword, etc. should begin on an odd-numbered page.   If necessary, leave the preceding page blank.

Foreword

A volume which belongs to a series or which is published under the auspices of an organization or Government department usually has a short foreword written by an official of the agency and giving essential information about the volume, the series, or both.

Preface

The author's preface should set forth the purpose and scope of the work.   It should set forth not only the contribution aimed at, but also the limitations arising from the subject or the conditions under which research was conducted.

If important methodological issues are involved, the methods of research and the organization of the material in the volume should be explained.

If controversial questions are involved, it may be well to give all points of view and, if possible, the conclusions of the author.

In cases of plural authorship the preface will set forth all allocation of credits in terms of the authorship of specific portions of the volume. It is also proper to give credit in the preface to those who, though not mentioned on the title page, contributed incidentally to the research or writing. Acknowledgments may be made also to those who have made important contributions to the work by facilitating the gathering of information, or to those who have contributed materially to the processing of the volume.

The preface may call attention to the appendages of the volume which will be of help to the reader, such as glossary and bibliographical note, and may also explain any set of terms on concepts which are recurrent and of particular importance in the text.

The preface should be dated as of the time the manuscript is sent to the printer.

Tables

Use Arabic numerals for tables (except those run-in with the text).

Follow the number with an em dash and the title in initial caps; center short titles above the table. If a title requires two lines, extend the first line from margin to margin and center the second line below the first. If the title requires more than two lines, the second and succeeding lines should be indented slightly under the word *Table*.

Table 5—Distribution of Infantry OCS Quotas among Major
Categories, June 1944–February 1945

Give the date or period of time directly after the main words of the title, preceded by a comma unless part of the title.

Units of measure applicable to the entire table should be given directly below the title in parentheses and in upper and lower case, as *Millions of Dollars*. Units of measure applicable to only some of the columns of the table should be shown in the headings of the columns affected.

All columns, including the stub (left-hand column), should have headings, typed in initial caps.

Use boxed headings in tables having more than two columns. Use vertical lines for columns and horizontal lines at the top and bottom of the table, whenever there are boxed headings.

Use a series of double-spaced periods (leaders) extending from the stub of the table to two spaces from the first column of figures.

Set off each three digits in figures with commas. Do not leave blank spaces in columns of figures. Use zeros where data is applicable, otherwise use em dashes.

Place totals at top of columns added. Indent the word *Total,* with the first letter capitalized, from the left-hand margin.

Where space must be saved, abbreviate units of time, military units, rank, units of measurement. Omit periods in words so treated in standard or military practice. In each table, abbreviate consistently or not at all. Avoid symbols, such as % and the abbreviation of *number* in column headings.

Use letters (*a, b, c*) for footnotes of numbered tables. Use numbers, consecutive with footnotes in the text, for footnotes for run-in tables.

The footnote reference mark should follow titles, headings, and stub entries but precede numbers. Footnote symbols for an omitted figure should be placed in parentheses in the space normally occupied by the figure.

List the source of the data in the table directly below the footnotes, separated by a space. Follow the word *Source,* italicized, with a colon.

If a table continues beyond a single page, repeat the table number and the full title. Place the word *Continued,* italicized, after the title, from which it should be separated by an em dash.

Tables run-in with the text are not numbered or titled, but are introduced by a sentence of the text and a colon. Do not use boxed headings or rulings. Indent text tables 10 or more spaces from left- and right-hand margins, depending on the width of stub and columns.

Charts

Use Arabic numerals for charts in the text, Roman for those in the appendix.

Type titles, and indicate *Source* as for tables.

Use asterisks, daggers, and section marks for footnote reference rather than letters.

Maps

Type headings and titles of maps in solid caps, Roman.

Use Arabic numerals for black and white maps, Roman for colored maps.

Essential place names and topographic features mentioned in the text must be shown on the map which covers that portion of text.

Because the size of the printed map is limited, care must be taken to plan maps which do not require too large a cartographic canvas.

Illustrations

Do not number illustrations. All references should mention the title of the illustration and the page number, except when the illustration is adjacent to the reference.

Type captions in solid caps.

On the back of the photograph note the date on which it was taken, and source (Army, Air Force, Navy, Marine, Coast Guard, or other) with photo number and location.

The photographs should be obtained in duplicate and specifications given on the duplicate rather than on an overlay.

If single caption is used for two pictures, use *above* and *below*, in parentheses.

Abbreviate as in the text.

Credit for illustrations should follow list in front matter.

Appendixes

Letter appendixes, using capital letters.

Type headings and titles in initial caps, not italicized.

Place appendixes directly after the text portion of the volume.

Glossary

Each volume should include an alphabetized glossary of the abbreviations used. The glossary and ensuing supplementary features follow the appendixes.

It is unnecessary to include abbreviations which are obvious, such as V-E Day and GHQ.

Map Symbols

Include a list of basic military symbols in each combat volume.

Bibliographical Note

General

Each volume should contain a bibliographical note, appraising the value and reliability of the sources.

Combat histories may find it useful to have the following sections: Manuscript Histories, Army Records, Navy Records, Marine Corps Records, Enemy Records, Interviews, Published Works.

If the bibliographical note contains a statement that Department of the Army records comprise the main source for the study, those records do not need to be listed individually.

Form

Books:

    Author, last name first (but Smith, John, and Bill Jones), period

    Title, in italics, period

    Supplementary note, if necessary, period

    Series and number, if any and if significant, period

    Edition, if other than first, semicolon

    Place of publication, comma

    Date, period

    Number of volumes, period

Examples:

    Ganoe, William A. *The History of the United States Army.* Rev. ed.; New York, 1943.

    UNITED STATES ARMY IN WORLD WAR II.

        Palmer, Robert R., Bell I. Wiley, and William R. Keast. *The Procurement and Training of Ground Combat Troops.* Washington, 1948.

    UNITED STATES ARMY IN WORLD WAR, 1917–1919: *Reports of Commander-in-Chief, A.E.F., Staff Sections and Services.* Washington, 1948. XIV.

Periodicals:

    Author, last name first, period

    Article title, comma, in quotes

    Periodical title, italicized, comma

    Volume number, usually Roman

    Date of issue, in parentheses, comma

    Page reference, period

Example:

    Miller, John Jr. "Crisis on Guadalcanal," *Military Affairs,* XI (1947), 195–212.

Chronology

A chronology of events or of operations is frequently of great value to a military student. This is especially true in complicated affairs and in farflung operations when it may be essential to keep in mind contemporaneous events bearing upon the problem.

The Index

General

A properly prepared and complete index is an essential part of all military histories. Without it, a work is of limited value to military men who may have need of the information contained therein. A trained military man or the author is best-qualified to prepare an index suitable for the needs of the service.

Form

Capitalize the initial letter of the first word of each main entry but not the first letter of a subheading; otherwise the general rules for capitalization apply to the index.

Write out first elements in a main entry, abbreviate second elements of a main entry and all elements of subentries, in accordance with standard Army practice and *Webster's International Dictionary*. Abbreviate U. S. as an adjective.

Use a colon to separate entries from page numbers, and commas to separate page numbers from each other. Numbers referring to material of a general nature which does not fit into the subheadings should immediately follow the main entry. Use an en dash to connect compound page numbers.

Do not use periods in the index except for abbreviations and to set off complete statements; use periods before and after statements beginning with *See* and *See also*.

When *See also* is followed by reference to several entries, use semicolons to separate items.

Italicize: *See* and *See also;* the names of ships; the names of enemy units; other terms which are italicized in the text.

Entries and subentries should preferably not start with prepositions; if prepositions are unavoidable they should not be considered in alphabetizing.

APPENDIX B
BIBLIOGRAPHIES

Note. The bibliographical aids, books, publications, and source material listed in this appendix contain many references to additional works or source material. The researcher and student of American military history will find the lists useful as a beginning. A similar list of works which influenced German military thinking was prepared by former Chief of Staff Franz Halder and others under the supervision of Historical Division, USAREUR. It was edited and reproduced by Foreign Studies Branch, OCMH, DA, under the title of "Brief Survey of German Military Literature."

Section I. BASIC WORKS BEARING ON MILITARY PROBLEMS

Ardant DuPicq. *Battle Studies.* Translated by John N. Greely and Robert C. Cotton. New York, 1921.

Bernhardi, Friedrich von. *On War To-day.* Translated by Karl von Donat. London, 1913. 2 vols.

Birnie, Arthur. *The Art of War.* London, 1942.

Bowman, Isaiah. *The New World, Problems in Political Geography.* Yonkers-on-the-Hudson, New York and Chicago, 1928.

Brodie, Bernard. *Sea Power in the Machine Age.* Princeton, 1941.

Burchardt, Jacob. *Force and Freedom: Reflections on History.* New York, 1943.

Clausewitz, Carl von. *On War.* Translated by J. J. Graham. London, 1918. 3 vols.

Colby, Elbridge. *Masters of Mobile Warfare.* Princeton, 1943.

Constitution of the United States of America.

DeGaulle, Charles. *The Army of the Future.* Philadelphia and New York, 1941.

De Vattel. *The Law of Nations.* Translated by Joseph Chitty. Philadelphia, 1863.

Douhet, Giulio. *The Command of the Air.* Translated by Ferrari. New York, 1942.

Earle, Edward M., Gordon A. Craig, and Felix Gilbert. *Makers of Modern Strategy.* Princeton, 1943.

Emeny, Brooks. *The Strategy of Raw Materials.* New York, 1934.

Erfurth, Waldemar. *Surprise.* Translated by Stefan T. Possony and Daniel Vilfroy. Harrisburg, 1943.

Foch, Ferdinand. *The Principles of War.* Translated by Belloc. New York, 1920.

Freytag-Loringhoven, Hugo, Freiherr von. *The Power of Personality in War.* Translated by Oliver L. Spaulding, 1938. Harrisburg, 1955.

Fuller, J. F. C.   *Armament and History.*   New York, 1945.

————.   *The Foundation of the Science of War.*   London, 1925.

————.   *Machine Warfare.*   London, 1942.

————.   *War and Western Civilization, 1832–1932.*   London, 1932.

Goltz, Baron Colmar von der.   *The Conduct of War.*   Translated by Joseph T. Dickman.   Kansas City, 1896.

————.   *The Nation in Arms.*   Translated by Philip A. Ashworth.   London, 1913.

Grotius, Hugo.   *The Law of War and Peace.*   Translated by Louise R. Loomis.   New York, 1949.

Hamilton, Sir Ian.   *Soul and Body of an Army.*   London, 1921.

Henderson, George F. R.   *The Science of War.*   New York, 1905.

Herring, Pendleton.   *The Impact of War.*   New York, 1941.

Jomini, Henry.   *The Art of War.*   Translated by G. H. Mandel and W. T. Craighill.   Philadelphia, 1862, 1863, 1879.

Kingston-McCloughry, E. J.   *War in Three Dimensions.*   London, 1949.

Lea, Homer.   *The Valor of Ignorance.*   New York, 1942.

Le Bon, Gustave.   *The Crowd: A Study of the Popular Mind.*   London, 1921.

Machiavelli, Niccolo.   *The Art of War.*   Albany, 1815.

————.   *The Prince and the Discourses.*   New York, 1940.

Mackinder, Sir Halford J.   *Democratic Ideals and Reality.*   New York, 1942.

Mahan, Alfred T.   *The Influence of Sea Power Upon History, 1660–1783.*   Boston, 1890.

Mahan, D. H.   *Advanced-Guard, Out-Post, and Detachment Service of Troops, with Essential Principles of Strategy and Grand Tactics.*   New York, 1864 and a number of editions from 1847 to 1864.

Montross, Lynn.   *War Through the Ages.*   New York, 1944.

Nef, John U.   *War and Human Progress.*   Cambridge, Mass., 1950.

Nickerson, Hoffman.   *The Armed Horde, 1793–1939.*   New York, 1940.

Oman, C. W. C.   *The Art of War in the Middle Ages.*   Revised and edited by John H. Beeler.   Ithaca, 1953.

Pratt, Edwin A.   *The Rise of Rail-Power in War and Conquest, 1833–1914.*   London, 1915 and 1916.

Reinhardt, G. C. and W. R. Kintner.   *Atomic Weapons in Land Combat.*   Harrisburg, 1953.

Robinett, Paul M. (ed.).   *Preparation for Leadership in America.*   Washington, 1950.

Schellendorff, Bronsart von.   *The Duties of The General Staff.*   4th ed.; London, 1905.

Seeckt, Hans von.   *Thoughts of a Soldier.*   Translated by G. Waterhouse.   London, 1930.

Simonds, Frank, and Brooks Emeny.   *The Great Powers in World Politics.*   New York, 1939.

Smith, Louis.   *American Democracy and Military Power, A Study of Civil Control of the Military Power in the United States.*   Chicago, 1951.

Spaulding, Oliver L., Hoffman Nickerson, and John W. Wright.   *Warfare: A Study of Military Methods from the Earliest Times.*   New York, 1925.

Spykman, Nicholas J. *America's Strategy in World Politics.* New York, 1942.

Stevens, William O. and Allan Wescott. *A History of Sea Power.* New York, 1942.

Sun Tzu. *The Art of War.* Translated by Lionel Giles. Harrisburg, 1944.

Thompson, Warren S. *Plenty of People.* New York, 1948.

Thucydides. *Complete Writing: The Peloponnesian War: The Unabridged Crawley Translation.* New York, 1934.

Turner, Gorden B. (ed.). *A History of Military Affairs in Western Society Since the Eighteenth Century.* Princeton, 1952. 32 vols.

United States Army. FM 22–10, *Leadership.* Washington, 1948.

U. S. Military Academy. *Summaries of Selected Military Campaigns.* West Point, 1953.

Vagts, Alfred. *History of Militarism.* New York, 1937.

Verdy du Vernois, Julius A. F. W. von. *Studies in the Leading of Troops.* Translated by William Gerlach. Kansas City, 1906.

Washington, George. *Washington's Farewell Address.* Privately printed for Veterans of Foreign Wars, 1926.

Wilkinson, Spenser. *The Brain of an Army.* 2d ed.; London, 1913.

Wright, Quincy. *A Study of War.* Chicago, 1942. 2 vols.

Zimmerman, Eric W. *World Resources and Industries.* New York, 1931.

Section II. SOURCE MATERIAL FOR THE WRITING OF AMERICAN MILITARY HISTORY: GENERAL WORKS

Bibliographies

Allied Geographical Section, Southwest Pacific Area. *Annotated Bibliography of the Southwest Pacific and Adjacent Areas.* Official Publication. General Headquarters Southwest Pacific, 1944. 3 vols.

Beers, Henry P. *Bibliographies in American History.* New York, 1942. This work describes general bibliographical aids. Chapter VIII, pp. 203–10, of Beers' work is devoted to military and naval history.

Bemis, Samuel F., and Grace G. Griffin. *Guide to the Diplomatic History of the United States, 1775–1921.* Washington, 1935.

Besterman, Theodore. *A World Bibliography of Bibliographies.* London, 1947.

Carnegie Institution of Washington. *Publication in History, Economics, and History of Science.* Reprinted from *Catalogue of Publications,* 1948.

Channing, Edward, Frederick J. Turner, and Albert B. Hart. *Guide to the Study and Reading of American History.* Boston, 1912. Although somewhat outdated, it contains an immense amount of highly organized information on sources of all sorts and is actually much more than a bibliography.

Coulter, Edith M., and Melanie Gerstenfield. *Historical Bibliographies.* Berkeley, 1935. A systematic and annotated guide with supplements.

Dutcher, George M., and others. *Guide to Historical Literature.* New York, 1931. This guide gives a selected, classified, and critical bib-

390016 O - 56 - 8

liography of the entire field of history, and includes special sections on military history.

Frank, Emma L. *Chaplaincy in the Armed Forces: A Preliminary Bibliography.* Oberlin, 1945.

Fuller, Grace H. *Demobilization: A Selected List of References.* Washington, 1945.

————. *Military Government: A List of References.* Washington, 1944.

General Service Schools. *Library Catalogue, 1927.* Fort Leavenworth, 1927. This work, with a 1929 supplement, lists 55,600 books, pamphlets, and documents, and 1,160 maps and atlases.

Griffin, Appleton P. C. (comp.). *Bibliography of American Historical Societies.* American Historical Association Annual Report for 1905. Washington, 1907.

Griffin, Grace G., and others (comp.). *Writings in American History.* Washington, 1908–.

Herring, Pendleton and others. *Civil-Military Relations.* Chicago, 1940.

Kirk, Grayson, and Richard P. Stebbins. *War and National Policy: A Syllabus.* New York, 1942.

Lanza, Conrad H. *List of Books on Military History and Related Subjects.* 3d ed.; Fort Leavenworth, Kansas, 1923.

Larned, J. N. *The Literature of American History: A Bibliographical Guide.* Boston, 1902. This work differs from Beers' in that it gives a brief description and evaluation of each work listed. The introduction contains information about records of each state. It has been extended by supplements to 1904.

Lauterbach, Alfred T., and others. "Modern War—Its Economic and Social Aspects." Princeton, 1942. A mimeographed listing of books in English, German, and French relating to warfare on the national level.

Matteson, David M. *General Index to Papers and Annual Reports of the American Historical Association, 1884–1914.* American Historical Association Annual Report for 1914. Washington, 1918.

Poore, Benjamin P. *A Descriptive Catalogue of the Government Publications of the United States, 1774–1881.* Washington, 1885.

Riling, Ray. *Guns and Shooting, a Bibliography.* New York, 1951.

Sabin, Joseph, and others. *A Dictionary of Books Relating to America.* New York, 1868.

Smith, Bruce L., and others. *Propaganda, Communication, and Public Opinion, a Comprehensive Reference Guide.* Princeton, 1946.

Social Science Research Council. *Civil Military Relations: An Annotated Bibliography 1940–1952.* New York, 1954.

Spaulding, Thomas M., and Louis C. Karpinski. *Early Military Books in the University of Michigan Libraries.* Ann Arbor, 1941.

Thompson, James W. *A History of Historical Writings.* New York, 1942.

United States Field Artillery School. *Officers Reserve Corps, A Bibliography.* Fort Sill, 1946.

U. S. Government Printing Office. *Checklist of U. S. Documents, 1789–1909.* Washington, 1911.

U. S. Military Academy. *Catalogue of the Library.* Supps. to 1881. Newburgh and Poughkeepsie, 1873–82.

U. S. War Department, Adjutant General's Office, Military Intelligence Division. *Sources of Information on Military Professional Subjects: A Classified List of Books and Publications.* Washington, 1898.

General Reference Works

American History

Adams, James T. (ed.). *Album of American History.* New York, 1946. 5 vols.

―――. *Dictionary of American History.* New York, 1940. 5 vols.

Adams, James T. *Atlas of American History.* New York, 1943.

Butterfield, Roger. *The American Past.* New York, 1947.

Crittenden, C. C., and Doris Godard. *Historical Societies in the United States and Canada.* Washington, 1944.

Fox, Dixon R. *Harper's Atlas of American History.* New York, 1920.

Johnson, Allen and Dumas Malone (eds.). *Dictionary of American Biography.* New York, 1928–44. 20 vols., index and supplement. This work lists sources.

Keller, Helen R. *Dictionary of Dates.* New York, 1934. 2 vols.

Langer, William L. *An Encyclopedia of World History.* Boston, 1950.

Larned, Josephus N. *New Larned History for Ready Reference, Reading, and Research.* Rev. ed.; Springfield, Mass., 1922–24. 12 vols. Alphabetical dictionary of universal history.

Lord, Clifford L., and Elizabeth H. *Historical Atlas of the United States.* New York, 1944.

National Cyclopaedia of American Biography. New York, 1892–1938. 32 vols.

Paullin, Charles, and John R. Wright. *Atlas of the Historical Geography of the United States.* New York, 1932.

Statesman's Year Book. London and New York, 1864–.

U. S. Bureau of the Census. *Historical Statistics of the United States, 1789–1945.* Washington, 1949.

U. S. Congress. *Official Congressional Directory of the American Congress.* Washington, 1809–. This is the standard reference book on members of Congress and, in recent years, a useful guide to governmental agencies. The official *Biographical Directory of the American Congress, 1774–1927,* Washington, 1928, is also valuable in this connection.

Who's Who in America. Chicago, 1889–. Revised and reissued biennially. The entries are prepared by biographees themselves.

Who Was Who in America. Chicago, 1942. A companion volume to *Who's Who in America* containing the biographies of deceased Americans who have appeared in the latter work since 1897 with dates of death added.

American Military History Combined with Military Dictionaries and Encyclopedias

The following compilations contain military biographies of Continental and Regular Army officers, 1775–1950, and other useful data on military organizations and battles.

Cullum, George W. *Biographical Register of the Officers and Graduates of the U. S. Military Academy.* Boston, 1891–1930. 7 vols.

Duane, William. *A Military Dictionary.* Philadelphia, 1810.

Farrow, Edward S. *Military Encyclopedia.* New York, 1885. 3 vols.

————. *Dictionary of Military Terms.* Rev. ed.; New York, 1918. This work is useful for the World War I period.

Garber, Max. *A Modern Military Dictionary.* 2d ed.; Washington, 1942.

Gaynor, Frank. *Military and Naval Dictionary.* New York, 1951.

Hamersly, Thomas H. S. *Complete Army and Navy Register of the United States of America from 1776 to 1887.* New York, 1888.

Heitman, Francis B. *Historical Register of Officers of the Continental Army.* Rev. ed.; Washington, 1914.

————. *Historical Register and Dictionary of the United States Army.* Washington, 1900. 2 vols.

Scott, H. L. *Military Dictionary,* New York, 1861. This is especially useful for the early period of the Civil War.

U. S. Army:

   Decorations United States Army 1862–1926. (With supplements I–V.) Washington, 1927–35.

   Official Army and Air Force Register. Washington, published annually until 1949. Following 1949 Army and Air Force registers are separate publications.

   The Medal of Honor of the United States Army. Washington, 1948.

U. S. Navy:

   Register of Commissioned and Warrant Officers of the United States Navy and Marine Corps. Washington, published annually.

   Wilhelm, Thomas. *A Military Dictionary and Gazetteer.* Rev. ed.; Philadelphia, 1881.

General Works

Secondary Works

Bailey, Thomas A. *A Diplomatic History of the American People.* New York, 1950.

Bancroft, George H. *History of the United States of America.* Boston, 1876. 6 vols.

Bemis, S. F. *A Diplomatic History of the United States.* New York, 1950.

Bemis, S. F. (ed.). *The American Secretaries of State and Their Diplomacy.* New York, 1927–29. 10 vols.

Brebner, John B. *The North Atlantic Triangle: The Interplay of Canada, the United States, and Great Britain.* New Haven, 1945.

Brown, Ralph H. *Historical Geography of the United States.* New York, 1948.

Channing, Edward A. *History of the United States.* New York, 1905–25. 6 vols.

Corwin, Edward S. *The President, Office and Powers.* New York, 1940.

———. *President's Control of Foreign Relations.* Princeton, 1917.

Gabriel, Ralph E. (ed.). *Pageant of America.* New Haven, 1925–29. 15 vols. The first of the large illustrated American histories.

Hart, Albert B. (ed.). *The American Nation.* New York, 1904–18. 28 vols.

Johnson, Allen, and others (eds.). *The Chronicles of America.* New Haven, 1918–50. 56 vols.

MacMaster, John B. *History of the People of the United States 1783–1865.* New York, 1895–1913. 8 vols.

Oberholtzer, E. P. *History of the United States, 1865–1901.* New York, 1917–37. 5 vols.

Paxon, Frederick L. *History of the American Frontier, 1763–1893.* Boston, 1924.

Perkins, Dexter. *Hands Off: A History of the Monroe Doctrine.* Boston, 1941.

Rhodes, James F. *History of the United States Since the Compromise of 1850.* New York, 1895–1929. 9 vols.

Savage, Carlton. *The Policy of the U. S. Toward Neutral Rights in Maritime Commerce in War, 1776–1914.* Washington, 1936. 2 vols.

Schlesinger, Arthur M., and Dixon R. Fox (eds.). *A History of American Life, 1492–1928.* New York, 1927–31. 12 vols.

Stephens, W. H., and E. M. Coulter (eds.). *The History of the South.* Baton Rouge, 1947–. 10 vols.

Tate, Merge. *The United States and Armaments.* Cambridge, 1948.

Winsor, Justin (ed.). *Narrative and Critical History of America.* Boston, New York, 1884–89. 8 vols.

Printed Sources

Earle, Edward M. (ed.). *The Federalist–.* New York, 1941.

Malloy, W. M., and Charles Garfield (eds.). *Treaties . . . Between the United States of America and Other Powers, 1776–1923.* Washington, 1916–23.

Miller, Hunter (ed.). *Treaties and Other International Acts of United States of America.* Washington, 1931–.

Richardson, James D. (comp.). *A Compilation of the Messages and Papers of the Presidents, 1789–1904.* Washington, 1896–1904. 10 vols.

U. S. Government:
 Annals of Congress, 1789–1824. Washington, 1825–37. 42 vols.
 Register of Debates in Congress, 1824–1837. Washington, 1825–37. 20 vols.
 Congressional Globe, 1833–1873. Washington, 1834–73. 111 vols.
 Congressional Record, 1874–. Washington, 1874–.
 Journal of the Executive Proceedings of the Senate of the U. S., 1789–1901. Washington, 1909. 34 vols.

Special Military Works

Secondary Works

Albion, Robert G. and Jennie B. Pope. *Sea Lanes in Wartime: The Amer ican Experience, 1775-1942.* New York, 1942.

Army War College. *Statement of a Proper Military Policy for the United States.* Washington, 1916.

Beckwith, Edmund, and others. *Lawful Action of State Military Forces* New York, 1944.

Berdahl, Clarence A. *War Powers of the Executive in the United States* Urbana, 1921.

Bernardo, C. Joseph and Eugene H. Bacon. *American Military Policy, It. Development Since 1775.* Harrisburg, 1955.

Birkhimer, William E. *Historical Sketch of the Organization, Administration Materiel and Tactics of the Artillery, United States Army.* Washington 1884.

Blakeslee, Fred G. *Uniforms of the World.* New York, 1929.

Brackett, Albert G. *History of the United States Cavalry.* New York, 1865

Carter, William G. H. *The American Army.* Indianapolis, 1915.

Castles, William T., and V. F. Kimball. *Firearms and Their Use.* Brook lyn, 1942.

Cloke, Harold E. *Condensed Military History of the United States.* Cam bridge, 1928.

Davis, George B. *A Treatise on the Military Law of the United States.* New York, 1915.

Dolph, Edward A. *Sound Off.* New York, 1942.

Dowell, Cassius M. *Military Aid to the Civil Power.* Ft. Leavenworth 1925.

Duggan, Joseph C. *The Legislative and Statutory Development of the Federa Concept of Conscription for Military Service.* Washington, 1946.

Dupuy, R. Ernest. *Men of West Point.* New York, 1951.

Falls, Cyril. *A Hundred Years of War.* London, 1953.

Forman, Sidney. *West Point: A History of the United States Military Acad emy.* New York, 1950.

Fuller, J. F. C. *Decisive Battles of the U. S. A.* New York, 1942.

———. *Armament and History.* New York, 1945.

Ganoe, William A. *History of the United States Army.* Rev. ed.; New York and London, 1942.

Glasson, William H. *Federal Military Pensions in the United States.* New York, 1918.

Gluckman, Arcadi. *United States Muskets, Rifles and Carbines.* Buffalo 1948.

Great Britain War Office. *Textbook of Small Arms.* London, 1929.

Halleck, W. Wager. *Military Art and Science.* New York, 1846.

Herr, John K., and Edward S. Wallace. *The Story of the U. S. Cavalry, 1775-1942.* Boston, 1953.

Heigl, Fritz. *Taschenbuch der Tanks.* Munich, 1930.

Hicks, James E. *Notes on United States Ordnance.* Mount Vernon, N. Y., 1940. 2 vols.

Hittle, J. D. *The Military Staff.* Harrisburg, 1949.

Huidekoper, Frederic L. *The Military Unpreparedness of the United States.* New York, 1915.

Ingersoll, L. D. *A History of the War Department of the United States.* Washington, 1879.

Jane, Fred T. *Jane's All the World's Aircraft.* New York, published since 1909.

———. *Jane's Fighting Ships.* New York, published since 1897.

Johnston, Robert M. *Leading American Soldiers.* New York, 1907.

Kerwin, Jerome G. *Civil-Military Relationship in American Life.* Chicago, 1948.

Knox, Dudley W. *A History of the United States Navy.* Rev. ed.; New York, 1948.

Liddell Hart, B. H. *Strategy: The Indirect Approach.* New York, 1954.

MacClay, E. S. *The History of the United States Navy.* New York, 1901–02. 3 vols.

Mathews, William, and Dixon Wecter. *Our Soldiers Speak, 1775–1918.* Boston, 1943.

Metcalf, C. H. *A History of the United States Marine Corps.* New York, 1939.

Munson, Edward L. Jr. *Leadership for American Army Leaders.* Washington, 1942.

National Geographic Society. *Insignia and Decorations of the U. S. Armed Forces.* Rev. ed.; Washington, 1944.

Newman, James R. *The Tools of War.* Garden City, 1942.

Palmer, John M. *America In Arms.* New Haven, 1941.

———. *Washington, Lincoln, Wilson: Three War Statesmen.* Garden City, 1930.

Palmer, Williston B. *The Evolution of the Military Policy of the United States.* Carlisle Barracks, 1946.

Pratt, Edward A. *The Rise of Rail-Power in War and Conquest, 1833–1914.* London, 1915 and 1916.

Pratt, Fletcher. *Eleven Generals: Studies in American Command.* New York, 1949.

———. *Short History of the Army and Navy.* Washington, 1944.

Puleston, William D. *Mahan: The Life and Work of Captain Alfred Mahan.* London, 1939.

Reichley, Marlin S. *Federal Military Intervention in Civil Disturbances.* Washington, 1939.

Rich, Bennett M. *The Presidents and Civil Disorder.* Washington, 1941.

Robinson, Fayette. *An Account of the Organization of the Army of the United States.* Philadelphia, 1848.

Rodenbough, Theophilus F., and William L. Haskins (eds.). *The Army of the United States, Historical Sketches of Staff and Line.* New York, 1896.

Root, Elihu. *The Military and Colonial Policy of the United States.* Cambridge, 1916.

Rossiter, Clinton. *The Supreme Court and the Commander in Chief.* Ithaca, 1950.

Senger u. Etterlin, Dr. F. v. *Taschenbuch der Panzer, 1943-1954.* Munich, 1954.

Smith, Louis. *American Democracy and Military Power: A Study of Civil Control of the Military Power in the United States.* Chicago, 1951.

Spaulding, Oliver L. *The United States Army in War and Peace.* New York, 1937.

Spears, John R. *The History of Our Navy, from Its Origin to the Present Day, 1775-1898.* New York, 1898. 5 vols.

Sprout, Harold H. and Margaret T. *The Rise of American Naval Power.* Princeton, 1942.

————. *Toward a New Order of Sea Power: American Naval Policy and the World Scene 1918-1922.* Princeton, 1943.

Steele, Matthew F. *American Campaigns.* Washington, 1901. 1 vol. text, 1 vol. maps.

Strait, N. A. *Alphabetical List of Battles 1754-1900.* Washington, 1901.

Thian, Raphael P. *Legislative History of the General Staff of the Army of the United States . . . 1775 to 1901.* Washington, 1901.

————. *Military Geography of the United States.* Washington, 1881.

Todd, Frederick P. and Fritz Kredel. *Soldiers of the American Army.* New York, 1954.

Upton, Emory. *The Military Policy of the United States.* Washington, 1917.

U. S. Army:
ROTCM 145-20 *American Military History: 1607-1953.* Washington, 1956.

Adjutant General's Office. *Federal Aid in Domestic Disturbances, 1787-1903.* Washington, 1903.

Inspector General's Office. *Regulations for Order and Discipline of Troops of the United States.* (General von Steuben's Blue Book.) Philadelphia, 1779.

Judge Advocate General's Department. *Federal Aid in Military Disturbances, 1903-1922.* Washington, 1922.

Office of Information. *The Army Almanac.* Washington,1951.

Office of the Chief of Military History:
The Army Lineage Books:
Vol. I–*Divisions and Higher Commands.*
Vol. II–*Infantry.* Washington, 1953.
Vol. III–*Armor.*
Vol. IV–*Field Artillery.*
Vol. V–*Antiaircraft Artillery.*
Vol. VI–*Corps of Engineers.*
Vol. VII–*Other Branches.*
Kreidberg, Lt. Col. Marvin A. and Lt. Merton G. Henry. *History of Military Mobilization in the United States Army.* Washington, 1956 (DA Pam 20-212).
Lerwill, Lt. Col. Leonard L. *The Personnel Replacement System in the United States Army.* Washington, 1954 (DA Pam 20-211).

Lewis, Lt. Col. George H. and Capt. John Mewha. *History of Utilization of Prisoners of War by the United States Army, 1776–1945.* Washington, 1955 (DA Pam 20–213).

Sparrow, Lt. Col. John C. *History of Personnel Demobilization in the United States Army.* Washington, 1952 (DA Pam 20–210).

The Quartermaster General. *Uniforms of the Army of the United States from 1774 to 1889.* Washington, 1908.

U. S. Marine Corps Historical Section. *One Hundred Eighty Landings of United States Marines, 1800–1934.* Washington, 1934. 2 vols.

U. S. Military Academy. *Campaign Summaries* [U. S.]. West Point, 1945–46. 2 vols.

U. S. Senate. *Politics of our Military National Defense.* (S. Doc. 274, 76th Cong., 3d sess.) Washington, 1940.

Vagts, Alfred. *History of Militarism.* New York, 1937.

Walton, William. *The Army and Navy of the United States* . . . . Boston, 1899–95. 2 vols.

Wecter, Dixon. *When Johnny Comes Marching Home.* Cambridge, Mass., 1944.

West, Richard S. *Admirals of the American Empire.* Indianapolis, 1948.

Westcott, Allan F. *American Sea Power Since 1775* . . . . Chicago, 1947.

White, Howard. *Executive Influence in Determining Military Policy in the United States.* Urbana, 1925.

Williams, Dion. *Army and Navy Uniforms and Insignia.* New York, 1918.

Wood, Leonard. *Our Military History: Its Facts and Fallacies.* Chicago, 1916.

Wyllie, Robert E. *Orders, Decorations and Insignia, Military and Civil.* New York, 1921.

Military Periodicals

A wealth of useful information relating to the Army and its activities, policies, development, administration, and operations will be found in the various service journals. They are valuable for contemporary opinions, events, technical and tactical developments, and biographical material.

Air Force Journal, 1946–; formerly *Air Corps Newsletter,* 1918–40; *Air Force,* 1940–42; and *Official Journal of the U. S. Air Force,* 1942–46.

Army Information Digest, 1945–. This official publication provides authoritative information on the policies, plans, and operations of the Department of the Army, the arms and services, and the reserve components.

Army Navy Air Force Journal, 1950–; formerly *Army Navy Journal,* 1863–1950. It is particularly valuable for material on contemporary matters of policy, organization, and current activity, opinion, and development in the Military Establishment. It also contains authoritative copies of documents, legislation, etc., affecting the Army. It is a valuable source of biographical material.

Army Navy Air Force Register, 1949–; formerly *Army Navy Register,* 1879–

1949. This publication is similar to the preceding journal and contains material of a like nature.

Journal of the Military Service Institution of the United States, vols. 1–61, 1879–1917. For a time this was the only American service journal. It is a good source for studying Army organization, institutions, and thinking within its period. Indexes cover volumes 1–34, 1879–1904, in volume 36; volumes 35–49, 1904–11, in volume 51; volumes 50–59, 1912–16, in volume 61.

Military Affairs, 1940–; formerly *Journal of the American Military History Foundation,* 1937–38, and *Journal of the American Military Institute,* 1939–40. This publication is devoted to military history with emphasis on American affairs.

The Military Review, 1932–; formerly *Review of Current Military Writing* 1921–32. This magazine publishes articles submitted by the faculty and students of the Army War College, the Command and General Staff College, and by authorities in all branches of the military art and science; digests leading articles found in foreign military publications; and contains a book review section. An index, published once each year, contains references to all articles other than book reviews.

Military and Naval Magazine of the United States. Washington, 1833–34. Vols. 1 and 2.

The service journals contain historical studies of importance to the arm or service concerned. Most significant are the various branch journals, some of which are listed with former titles as follows: *Army,* formerly *U. S. Army Combat Forces Journal,* 1950–56, combining the *Infantry Journal,* 1904–50, the *Field Artillery Journal,* 1910–50, and *Antiaircraft Journal,* 1948–55, formerly *Journal of United States Artillery,* 1892–1922, and *Coast Artillery Journal,* 1922–48; *Armor,* formerly *Cavalry Journal,* 1888–1946, and *Armored Cavalry Journal,* 1946–50; *Military Engineer,* formerly *Occasional Papers,* 1904–09, *Memoirs,* 1909–20; *Quartermaster Review,* 1921–; and *Ordnance,* formerly *Army Ordnance,* 1920–47.

National Rifle Association. *American Rifleman.* Washington, 1885–.
U. S. Naval Institute Procedings. Annapolis, 1874–.

Section III. SOURCE MATERIAL FOR THE WRITING OF AMERICAN MILITARY HISTORY: 1607–1775

Bibliographies

Beers, Henry P. "The Papers of the British Commanders in Chief in North America, 1754–1783," *Military Affairs,* Vol. XIII, No. 2, pp. 79–94.

Evans, Charles. *American Bibliography.* Chicago, 1903–34. 12 vols.

Hease, Adelaide R. "Materials for a Bibliography of the Public Archives of the 13 Original States, Covering the Colonial Period and the State Period to 1789." In American Historical Association *Report* for 1906, II, pp. 239–572.

General Works

Secondary Works

Andrews, C. M. *The Colonial Period of American History.* New Haven, 1934–. 4 vols.

Beers, George L. *The Origins of the British Colonial System.* New York, 1908.

———. *British Colonial Policy, 1754–1765.* New York, 1907.

Colby, Charles W. *The Fighting Governor.* (Chronicles of Canada). Toronto, 1915.

Graham, Gerald S. *Empire of the North Atlantic.* Toronto, 1950.

Marquis, T. G. *The War Chief of the Ottawas (Chronicles of Canada).* Toronto, 1915.

Osgood, Herbert L. *The American Colonies in the 17th Century.* New York, 1904. 3 vols.

———. *The American Colonies in the 18th Century.* New York, 1924. 4 vols.

Parkman, Francis. *The Conspiracy of Pontiac and the Indian War after the Conquest of Canada.* Boston, 1903.

———. *Count Frontenac and New France Under Louis XIV.* Boston, 1903.

———. *The Half Century of Conflict.* Boston, 1903.

———. *Montcalm and Wolfe.* Boston, 1903.

Raymond, Ethel T. *Tecumseh.* (Chronicles of Canada). Toronto, 1915.

Wood, Louis Aubrey. *The War Chief of the Six Nations.* (Chronicles of Canada). Toronto, 1915.

Wood, William C. H. *The Great Fortress.* (Chronicles of Canada). Toronto, 1915.

———. *The Passing of New France.* (Chronicles of Canada). Toronto, 1915.

———. *The Winning of Canada.* (Chronicles of Canada). Toronto, 1915.

———. *The Fight for Canada.* London, 1905.

Wong, George M. *The Fall of Canada.* Oxford, 1914.

Printed Sources

Archives of Maryland (1637–1784). Baltimore, 1883–.

Brock, R. A. (ed.). *The Official Records of Robert Dinwiddie . . . 1751–1758.* Richmond, 1883–84. 2 vols.

Browne, William H. (ed.) *Correspondence of Governor Horatio Sharpe, 1753–1771.* (Archives of Maryland). Vols. VI, IX, XIV, XXXI. Baltimore, 1888, 1895, 1911.

Callaghan, E. B., and B. Fernow (eds.). *Documents Relative to the Colonial History of the State of New York.* Albany, 1856–87. 15 vols.

Chandler, A. D. (comp.). *Colonial Records of Georgia.* Rev. and published by Lucian L. Knight. Atlanta, 1904–. 26 vols.

Fitzpatrick, John C. (ed.). *The Diaries of George Washington, 1748–1799.* Vol. I. Boston, 1925.

———. *The Writings of George Washington.* Vols. I–IV. Washington, 1931–40. Index in vols. XXXVIII–XXXIX.

Hazard, Samuel, and others (comp.). *Pennsylvania Archives, 1664–.* Philadelphia and Harrisburg, 1852–1907. 6 series, 91 vols.

Labaree, Leonard (ed.). *Royal Instructions to the British Colonial Governors, 1670–1776.* New York and London, 1935. 2 vols. See Labaree's: *Royal Government–.*

Saunders, W. L. (comp. and ed.). *Colonial Records of North Carolina.* Raleigh, 1886–90. 10 vols.

Wood, William C. H. (ed.). *The Logs of the Conquest of Canada.* Toronto, 1909.

Special Military Works

Secondary Works

Doddridge, John. *Notes on the Settlements and Indian Wars of the Western Parts of Virginia and Pennsylvania, 1763–1783.* Albany, 1876.

Freeman, Douglas S. *George Washington A Biography.* Vols. I and II. New York, 1948.

Historical Section of the General Staff. *The Local Forces of New France: The Militia of the Province of Quebec, 1763–1775.* (*A History of the Organization, Development and Services of the Military and Naval Forces of Canada from the Peace of Paris in 1763 to the Present Time.* Vol. I.) Ottawa, 1919.

Lincoln, C. H. *Narratives on the Indian Wars.* New York, 1913.

Long, John C. *Lord Jeffery Amherst, A Soldier of the King.* New York, 1933.

Pargellis, Stanley M. *Lord Loudoun in North America.* New Haven, 1933.

Peckham, Howard H. *Pontiac and the Indian Uprising.* Princeton, 1947.

Thwaites, R. G., and L. P. Kellogg (eds.). *Documentary History of Dunmore's War, 1774.* Madison, 1905.

Wade, Herbert T. *A Brief History of the Colonial Wars in America from 1607 to 1775.* New York, 1948.

Wertenbaker, Thomas J. *Torchbearer of the Revolution, the Story of Bacon's Rebellion and Its Leader.* Princeton, 1940.

Printed Sources

Carter, Clarence E. (ed.). *The Correspondence of General Thomas Gage, 1763–1775.* New Haven, 1931–33. 2 vols.

Knox, John. *An Historical Journal of the Campaign in North America for the Years 1757, 1758, 1759, 1760.* Toronto, 1914–16. 3 vols.

Myrand, Ernest. *1690: Sir William Phips Devant Québec.* Quebec, 1893.

Pargellis, Stanley M. (ed.). *Military Affairs in North America, 1748–1765* . . . . London and New York, 1936.

State of New York, Division of Archives and History. *Sir William Johnson Papers.* Albany, 1921 . . .

SOURCE MATERIAL FOR THE WRITING OF AMERICAN MILITARY HISTORY: 1775–1783

Bibliographies

Peckham, Howard H. (comp.).   *Guide to the Manuscript Collection in the William N. Clements Library.*   Ann Arbor, 1942.

U. S. National Park Service, Historical Division.   *A Bibliography of the Virginia Campaign and Siege of Yorktown, 1781.*   Yorktown, 1941.

General Works

Secondary Works

Bemis, Samuel F.   *The Diplomacy of the American Revolution.*   New York, 1935.

Burnett, Edmund C.   *The Continental Congress.*   New York, 1941.

Channing, Edward.   *History of the United States.*   Vol. III, 1761–1789. New York, 1912.

French, Allen.   *The First Year of the American Revolution.*   Boston, 1934.

Greene, Evarts B.   *The Revolutionary Generation: 1763–1790.*   New York, 1943.

Historical Section, Canadian General Staff.   *The War of the American Revolution: The Province of Quebec Under the Administration of Governor Sir Guy Carleton, 1775–1778.*   Ottawa, 1920.

Jensen, Merrill.   *The New Nation: A History of the United States During the Confederation, 1781–1789.*   New York, 1950.

Miller, John C.   *Triumph of Freedom, 1775–1783.*   Boston, 1948.

Trevelyan, Sir George O.   *The American Revolution.*   London, 1899–1907. 4 vols.

———.   *George the Third and Charles Fox—the Concluding Part of the American Revolution.*   London, 1912–14.   2 vols.

Van Tyne, Claude H.   *The War of Independence.*   Boston, 1929.

Printed Sources

Burnett, Edmund C. (ed.).   *Letters of Members of the Continental Congress.*   Washington, 1921–36.   8 vols.

Clark, Walter (comp. and ed.).   *State Records of North Carolina.*   Raleigh, 1890–.   16 vols.

Fitzpatrick, John C. (ed.).   *The Diaries of George Washington, 1748–1789.*   Boston, 1925, 2 vols.

———.   *The Writings of George Washington from the Original MS Sources, 1745–1799.*   Washington, 1931–44.   39 vols.   Index in vols. XXXVIII–XXXIX.

Force, Peter (ed.).   *American Archives.*   Washington, 1837–53.   4th and 5th Series, 9 vols.

Ford, Worthington C., and others (eds.).   *Journals of the Continental Congress.*   Washington, 1904–37.   34 vols.

Fortescue, John W. (ed.). *The Correspondence of King George the Third, from 1760 to December 1783.* London, 1927–28. 6 vols.

Wharton, Francis (ed.). *The Revolutionary Diplomatic Correspondence of th United States.* Washington, 1889. 6 vols.

Special Military Works

Secondary Works

Adams, Charles F. *Studies Military and Diplomatic, 1775–1865.* Nev York, 1911.

Adams, Randolph G. *Lexington to Fallen Timbers, 1775–1794.* Ann Ar bor, 1942.

Alden John R. *General Gage in America, Being Principally his Role in th American Revolution.* Baton Rouge, 1948.

Allen, Gardner W. *A Naval History of the American Revolution.* Boston 1913. 2 vols.

Anderson, Troyer S. *The Command of the Howe Brothers during the Ameri can Revolution.* New York, 1936.

Balch, Thomas. *The French in America during the War of Independence 1777–1783.* Philadelphia, 1891–95. 2 vols.

Belcher, Henry. *The First American Civil War.* London, 1911. 2 vols

Bennett, Clarence E. *Advance and Retreat to Saratoga.* Schenectady 1927. 2 vols.

Bill, Alfred H. *The Campaign of Princeton, 1776–1777.* Princeton, 1948

Bolton, Charles K. *The Private Soldier under Washington.* New York 1902.

Bonsol, Stephen. *When the French were here . . . the French Forces i America, and their Contribution to the Yorktown Campaign.* New York 1945.

Bowman, Allen. *The Morale of the American Revolutionary Army.* Wash ington, 1943.

Boyd, Thomas A. *Light-Horse Harry Lee.* New York, 1931.

———. *Mad Anthony Wayne.* New York, 1929.

Brooks, Noah. *Henry Knox.* New York, 1900.

Butterfield, Consul W. *History of Lt. Col. George Rogers Clark's Conquest the Illinois and of the Wabash Towns.* Columbus, 1903.

Carrington, Henry B. *Washington, the Soldier.* New York, 1899.

Codman, John. *Arnold's Expedition to Quebec.* Tarrytown, 1901.

Cronau, Rudolf. *The Army of the American Revolution and Its Organize* New York, 1923.

Curtis, Edward E. *Organization of the British Army in the American Revol tion.* New Haven, 1926.

Daves, Edward G. *Maryland and North Carolina in the Campaign of 1780 1781.* Baltimore, 1893.

Dean, Sydney W. *Fighting Dan of the Long Rifles.* Philadelphia, 1942

De Fonblanque, Edward B. *Political and Military Episodes . . . Deriv from the Life and Correspondence of . . . John Burgoyne.* London, 187

Eelking, Max von. *The German Allied Troops in the North American War Independence.* Translated and abridged by J. D. Rosengarte

Albany, 1893.

English, William H. *Conquest of the Country Northwest of the River Ohio, 1778-1783; and Life of General George Rogers Clark.* Indianapolis, 1896. 2 vols.

Field, Thomas W. *The Battle of Long Island.* Brooklyn, 1869.

Fitzpatrick, John C. *The Spirit of the Revolution.* Boston, 1924.

Fortescue, Sir John W. *A History of the British Army.* Vol. III, 1763-1793. London, 1899-1930.

Freeman, Douglas S. *George Washington.* Vols. I-V. New York, 1948-.

French, Allen. *The Siege of Boston.* New York, 1911.

Frothingham, Thomas G. *Washington, Commander-in-Chief.* Boston, 1930.

Fuller, John F. C. *British Light Infantry in the Eighteenth Century.* London, 1925.

Gottschalk, Louis R. *Lafayette Joins the American Army.* Chicago, 1937.

———. *Lafayette and the Close of the American Revolution.* Chicago, 1942.

Greene, Francis V. *The Revolutionary War and the Military Policy of the United States.* New York, 1911.

Greene, George W. *Life of Major General Nathanael Greene.* New York, 1867-71. 3 vols.

Haiman, Miecislaus. *Kosciuszko in the American Revolution.* New York, 1943.

Hatch, Louis C. *The Administration of the American Revolutionary Army.* New York, 1904.

Henderson, Archibald. *The Conquest of the Old Southwest.* New York, 1920.

Huddleston, Francis J. *Gentleman Johnny Burgoyne.* Indianapolis, 1927.

James, James A. *The Life of George Rogers Clark.* Chicago, 1928.

James, William M. *The British Navy in Adversity: A Study of the War of American Independence.* New York, 1926.

Johnson, Victor L. *The Administration of the American Commissariat during the Revolutionary War.* Philadelphia, 1941.

Johnson, William. *Sketches of the Life and Correspondence of Nathanael Greene.* Charleston, 1822. 2 vols.

Johnston, Henry P. *The Campaign of 1776 Around New York and Brooklyn.* Brooklyn, 1878.

———. *The Yorktown Campaign.* New York, 1881.

Kapp, Friedrich. *Life of Frederick William von Steuben.* New York, 1859.

Keim, DeB. Randolph. *Rochambeau.* (U. S. Gen Doc 537, 59th Cong., 1st sess.). Washington, 1907.

Knox, Dudley W. *The Naval Genius of George Washington.* Boston, 1932.

Landers, Howard E. L. *Virginia Campaign and Blockade and Siege of Yorktown.* Washington, 1931.

Lefferts, Charles M. *Uniforms of the American, British, French and German Armies . . . the American Revolution, 1775-1783.* New York, 1926.

Lewis, Charles L. *Admiral de Grasse and American Independence.* Annapolis, 1945.

Lossing, Benson J. *The Pictorial Field-Book of the Revolution.* New York, 1851–52. 2 vols.

Lowell, Edward J. *The Hessians and Other German Auxiliaries of Great Britain in the Revolutionary War.* New York, 1884.

Lundin, Leonard. *Cockpit of the Revolution: The War for Independence in New Jersey.* Princeton, 1940.

Maclay, Edgar S. *A History of American Privateers.* New York, 1924.

Mahan, Alfred T. *The Influence of Sea Power upon History, 1660–1783.* Boston, 1890.

———. *Major Operations of the Navies in the War of American Independence.* Boston, 1913.

Marshall, John. *The Life of George Washington.* Fredericksburg, 1926. 5 vols.

Martyn, Charles. *The Life of Artemus Ward.* New York, 1921.

McCrady, Edward. *The History of South Carolina in the Revolution.* New York, 1901.

McMunn, Sir George F. *The American War of Independence in Perspective.* London, 1939.

Montross, Lynn. *Rag, Tag and Bobtail, the Story of the Continental Army, 1775–1783.* New York, 1952.

Moore, Howard P. *The Life of General John Stark.* New York, 1949.

Nickerson, Hoffman. *The Turning Point of the Revolution.* Boston, 1928.

Palmer, John M. *General von Steuben.* New Haven, 1937.

Patterson, Samuel W. *Horatio Gates.* New York, 1941.

Paullin, Charles O. *The Navy of the American Revolution.* Cleveland, 1906.

Preston, John H. *A Gentleman Rebel: The Exploits of Anthony Wayne.* New York, 1930.

Roberts, Kenneth. *March to Quebec.* New York, 1938.

Schermerhorn, Frank E. *American and French Flags of the Revolution, 1775–1783.* Philadelphia, 1948.

Sherwin, Oscar. *Benedict Arnold, Patriot and Traitor.* New York, 1931.

Smith, Justin H. *Our Struggle for the Fourteenth Colony—Canada and the American Revolution.* New York, 1907. 2 vols.

Stedman, Charles. *The History of the Origin, Progress, and Termination of the American War.* London, 1794. 2 vols.

Stille, Charles J. *Major General Anthony Wayne and the Pennsylvania Line in the Continental Army.* Philadelphia, 1893.

Stone, William L. *Border Wars of the American Revolution.* New York, 1845. 2 vols.

———. *The Campaign of Lt. Gen. John Burgoyne.* Albany, 1877.

Stryker, William S. *The Battles of Trenton and Princeton.* Boston, 1898.

———. *The Battle of Monmouth.* Princeton, 1927.

Swiggett, Howard. *War out of Niagara: Walter Butler and the Tory Rangers.* New York, 1933.

Van Doren, Carl C. *Secret History of the American Revolution.* New York, 1941.

Wallace, Willard M. *Appeal to Arms—A Military History of the American Revolution.* New York, 1951.

Ward, Christopher. *War of the Revolution.* New York, 1952. 2 vols.
Wildes, Harry E. *Anthony Wayne.* New York, 1941.
———. *Valley Forge.* New York, 1938.
Winsor, Justin. *The American Revolution.* (*Narrative and Critical History of America,* Vol. VI.). Boston, 1884–89.
Wood, William. *The Winning of Freedom.* New Haven, 1927.

Printed Sources

Abbott, William (ed.). *Memoirs of Maj. Gen. William Heath* . . . . New York, 1901.
Andre, John. *Major Andre's Journal.* Tarryton, 1930.
Burgoyne, John. *A Statement of the Expedition from Canada, as Laid before the House of Commons.* London, 1780.
Connecticut Historical Society. *Orderly Book and Journals Kept by Connecticut Men . . . 1775–1778.* Hartford, 1899.
Eelking, Max von (ed.). *Memoirs and Letters and Journals of Major General Riedesel.* Translated by William L. Stone. Albany, 1868. 2 vols.
Egle, William H. (ed.). *Journals and Diaries of the War of the Revolution . . . 1775–1783.* Harrisburg, 1893.
Ford, Washington C. (ed.). *Defenses of Philadelphia in 1777.* Brooklyn, 1897.
Heitman, Francis B. *Historical Register of Officers of the Continental Army.* Washington, 1893.
Howe, Sir William. *Narrative . . . in a Committee of the House of Commons.* London, 1780.
———. *Orderly Book, 1775–6.* Edited by Benjamin F. Stevens. London, 1890.
Lee, Charles. *The Lee Papers, 1754–1811.* New York, 1872–75. 4 vols.
Lee, Henry. *Memoirs of the War in the Southern Department of the United States.* New York, 1869.
Linn, John B. (ed.). *Minutes of the Board of War . . . 1777 . . . and Other Papers Relating to the Revolutionary War.* Harrisburg, 1874.
Mackenzie, Frederick. *Diary . . . 1775–1781.* Cambridge, 1930. 2 vols.
Moultrie, William. *Memoirs of the American Revolution . . .* [in] *North and South Carolina, a d Georgia.* New York, 1802. 2 vols.
New York State, Division of Archives and History. *The Sullivan-Clinton Campaign of 1779. Chronology and Selected Documents.* Albany, 1929.
O'Callaghn, Edmund B. (ed.). *Orderly Book, Lt. Gen. John Burgoyne.* Albany, 1860.
Riedesel, Baroness Friederike. *Letters and Journals* . . . . Albany, 1867.
Roberts, Kenneth L. (ed.). *March to Quebec: Journals of the Members of Arnold's Expedition.* New York, 1938.
Saffell, William T. H. (comp.). *Records of the Revolutionary War.* New York, 1858.
Simes, Thomas. *Military Guide for Young Officers.* Philadelphia, 1776. 2 vols.
Steuben, Frederick W. von. *Regulations for the Order and Discipline of the Troops of the United States.* Philadelphia, 1779.

390016 O - 56 - 9

Stevens, Benjamin F. (ed.). *The Campaign in Virginia, 1781.* London, 1888. 2 vols.

Sullivan, John. *Letters and Papers of Maj. Gen. John Sullivan.* Edited by Otis G. Hammond. Concord, 1930–39. 3 vols.

Tarleton, Banastre. *History of the Campaigns of 1780–1781 in the Southern Provinces of North America.* London, 1787.

Uhlendorf, Bernhard A. (ed.). *The Siege of Charleston . . . Diaries and Letters of Hessian Officers.* Ann Arbor, 1938.

Weedon, George (ed.). *Valley Forge Orderly Book . . . .* New York, 1902.

Section V. SOURCE MATERIAL FOR THE WRITING OF AMERICAN MILITARY HISTORY: 1783–1861

Bibliographies

Haferkorn, Henry E. *The War with Mexico, 1846–1848: a Select Bibliography.* Washington, 1914.

General Works

Secondary Works

Adams, Henry. *History of the United States in the Administration of Jefferson and Madison.* New York, 1889–91. 9 vols.

Bassett, John S. *Life of Andrew Jackson.* New York, 1911. 2 vols.

Burt, Alfred L. *The United States, Great Britain, and British North America.* New Haven, 1940.

Corey, Albert B. *The Crisis of 1830–1842 in Canadian-American Relations.* New Haven, 1941.

Cox, Isaac J. *The West Florida Controversy, 1798–1813.* Baltimore, 1918.

DeVoto, Bernard. *The Year of Decision: 1846.* Boston, 1943.

Fuller, John D. P. *The Movement for the Acquisition of All Mexico, 1846–1848.* Baltimore, 1936.

Green, Thomas M. *The Spanish Conspiracy.* Cincinnati, 1891.

McCaleb, Walter F. *The Aaron Burr Conspiracy.* New York, 1903.

McCormac, Eugene I. *James K. Polk.* Berkeley, 1922.

Nichols, Roy F. *Franklin Pierce.* Philadelphia, 1931.

Parton, James. *Life of Andrew Jackson.* New York, 1860. 3 vols.

Pratt, Julius W. *Expansionists of 1812.* New York, 1925.

Rives, George L. *The United States and Mexico, 1821–1848.* New York, 1913. 2 vols.

Robertson, James A. *Louisiana Under the Rule of Spain, France, and the United States, 1785–1807.* Cleveland, 1911. 2 vols.

Roosevelt, Theodore. *The Winning of the West.* New York, 1889–96. 4 vols.

Tiffary, Orrin E. *Relations of the United States to the Canadian Rebellion of 1837–1838.* Westminster, Md., 1905.

Updyke, Frank A. *The Diplomacy of the War of 1812.* Baltimore, 1915.

Weinberg, Albert K. *Manifest Destiny.* Baltimore, 1935.
Whitaker, Arthur P. *The Mississippi Question, 1795–1803.* New York, 1934.
———. *The Spanish American Frontier, 1783–1795.* New York, 1927.
Wiltse, Charles M. *John C. Calhoun.* Indianapolis, 1944. 3 vols.
Worthan, Louis J. *History of Texas.* Fort Worth, 1924. 5 vols.

Printed Sources

Bassett, John S. (ed.). *Correspondence of Andrew Jackson.* Washington, 1926–35. 7 vols.
Carter, Clarence E. (ed.). *The Territorial Papers of the United States.* Washington, 1934–42. 10 vols.
Fitzpatrick, John C. (ed.). *The Writings of George Washington.* Vols. XXIV–XXXVII. Washington, 1931–40. Index in vols. XXXVIII–XXXIX.
. . . . *The Diaries of George Washington.* Vols. II–IV. Boston, 1925.
Hamilton, Stanislaus M. (ed.). *The Writings of James Monroe.* New York, 1898–1903. 7 vols.
Quaife, Milo M. (ed.). *The Diary of James K. Polk during his Presidency.* Chicago, 1910. 4 vols.
United States Government. *The Diplomatic Correspondence of the United States of America . . . 1783 . * . 1789.* 3d ed.; Washington, 1855. 3 vols.
———. *American State Papers.* Washington, 1832–61. 38 vols.
    Class I: *Foreign Relations.* 1789–1828. 6 vols.
    Class II: *Indian Affairs.* 1789–1827. 2 vols.
    Class IV: *Naval Affairs.* 1789–1836. 4 vols.
    Class V: *Military Affairs.* 1789–1838. 7 vols.
    Class IX: *Claims.* 1790–1823. 1 vol.

Special Military Works

Secondary Works

Adams, Henry. *The War of 1812.* Edited by Maj. H. A. DeWeerd. Washington, 1944.
Alcaraz, Ramon. *The Other Side: or Notes for the History of the War Between the United States and Mexico.* New York, 1850.
Allen, Gardner W. *Our Naval War with France.* Boston, 1909.
———. *Our Navy and the Barbary Corsairs.* Boston, 1905.
Babcock, Louis L. *The War of 1812 on the Niagara Frontier.* Buffalo, 1927.
Baldwin, Leland D. *Whiskey Rebels.* Pittsburgh, 1939.
Bandel, Eugene. *Frontier Life in the Army, 1854–1861.* Glendale, Calif., 1932.
Barnes, James. *Naval Actions of the War of 1812.* New York, 1896.
Barrows, Edward M. *Matthew Calbraith Perry.* Indianapolis, 1935.

Beers, Henry P. *The Western Military Frontier, 1815–1846.* Philadelphia, 1935.

Beirne, Francis F. *The War of 1812.* New York, 1949.

Bill, Alfred H. *Rehearsal for Conflict: The War with Mexico, 1846–1848.* New York, 1947.

Cleaves, Freeman. *Old Tippecanoe: William Henry Harrison and His Time.* New York, 1939.

Coggeshall, George. *History of American Privateers and Letters of Marque.* New York, 1856.

Cooke, Philip St. G. *Conquest of New Mexico and California.* New York, 1878.

Cranwell, John P. *Men of Marque: A History of Private Armed Vessels out of Baltimore during the War of 1812.* New York, 1940.

Cullum, George W. *Campaigns of the War of 1812–1815.* New York, 1879.

DePeyster, John W. *Personal and Military History of Philip Kearny.* New York, 1869.

Downe, Randolph C. *Council Fires on the Upper Ohio: A Narrative of Indian Affairs in the Upper Ohio Valley until 1795.* Philadelphia, 1940.

Dutton, Charles J. *Oliver Hazard Perry.* New York, 1935.

Dyer, Brainerd. *Zachary Taylor.* Baton Rouge, 1946.

Elliott, Charles W. *Winfield Scott, the Soldier and the Man.* New York, 1937.

Fortescue, Sir John W. *History of the British Army.* Vols. VIII–X (War of 1812). London, 1899–1930.

Goebel, Dorothy B. *William Henry Harrison.* Indianapolis, 1926.

Green, James A. *William Henry Harrison.* Richmond, 1941.

Hamilton, Holman. *Zachary Taylor, Soldier of the Republic.* Indianapolis, 1941.

Headley, Joel T. *The Second War with England.* New York, 1853. 2 vols.

Henry, Robert S. *The Story of the Mexican War.* Indianapolis, 1950.

Hughes, John T. *Doniphan's Expedition.* Cincinnati, 1848.

Ingersoll, Charles J. *Historical Sketch of the Second War Between the United States of America and Great Britain.* Philadelphia, 1845–52. 3 vols.

Jacobs, James R. *The Beginning of the U. S. Army, 1783–1812.* Princeton, 1947.

———. *Tarnished Warrior: Major General James Wilkinson.* New York, 1938.

James, Marquis. *Andrew Jackson: The Border Captain.* Indianapolis, 1933.

———. *The Raven: A Biography of Sam Houston.* Indianapolis, 1929.

James, William. *A Full and Correct Account of the Military Occurrences of the Late War Between Great Britain and the United States of America.* London, 1818. 2 vols.

Kearny, Thomas. *General Philip Kearny.* New York, 1937.

Lewis, Lloyd. *Captain Sam Grant.* Boston, 1950.

Lossing, Benson J. *The Pictorial Field Book of the War of 1812.* New York, 1868.

Lucas, Charles P. *The Canadian War of 1812.* Oxford, 1906.

Mahan, Alfred T.   *Sea Power in its Relation to the War of 1812.*   Baltimore, 1915.   2 vols.

Marine, William M.   *The British Invasion of Maryland.*   Baltimore, 1913.

McAfee, Robert B.   *History of the Late War in the Western Country . . . Tippecanoe to . . . New Orleans.*   Lexington, 1816.

Nevins, Allan.   *Fremont, The West's Greatest Adventurer.*   New York, 1928. 2 vols.

Pelzer, Louis.   *Marches of the Dragoons in the Mississippi Valley . . . 1813 . . . 1850.*   Iowa City, 1917.

Ripley, Roswell S.   *The War with Mexico.*   New York, 1849.   2 vols.

Roosevelt, Theodore.   *The Naval War of 1812.*   New York and London, 1927.

Smith, Justin H.   *The War with Mexico.*   New York, 1919.   2 vols.

Snider, C. H. J.   *Under the Red Jack: Privateers of the Maritime Provinces of Canada in the War of 1812.*   Toronto, 1928.

Steiner, B. C.   *The Life and Correspondence of James McHenry.*   Cleveland, 1907.

Stevens, Frank E.   *The Black Hawk War.*   Chicago, 1903.

Wallach, Sidney (ed.).   *Commodore Perry's Naval Expedition to the China Seas and Japan.*   New York, 1952.

Wesley, Edgar B.   *Guarding the Frontier . . . 1815 to 1825.*   Minneapolis, 1935.

Wilcox, Cadmers M.   *History of the Mexican War.*   Washington, 1892.

Williams, Alfred M.   *Sam Houston and the War of Independence in Texas.*   Boston, 1893.

Williams, John S.   *History of the Invasion and Capture of Washington.*   New York, 1857.

Wiltse, Charles M.   *John C. Calhoun, Nationalist 1782–1828.*   New York, 1944.

Wood, William C. H.   *The War with the United States.*   Toronto, 1915.

Young, Bennett H.   *The Battle of the Thames.*   Louisville, 1903.

Printed Sources

Anderson, Robert.   *An Artillery Officer in the Mexican War, 1846–1847.*   New York, 1911.

Armstrong, John.   *Notices of the War of 1812.*   New York, 1840.   2 vols.

Bandel, Eugene.   *Frontier Life in the Army, 1854–1861.*   Glendale, 1932.

Cooke, Philip St. G.   *Scenes and Adventures in the Army.*   Philadelphia, 1857.

Coues, Elliott (ed.).   *The Expedition of Zebulon Montgomery Pike.*   New York, 1895.   3 vols.

———.   *The Lewis and Clark Expedition.*   New York, 1893.

Cruikshank, E.   *The Documentary History of the Campaign upon the Niagara Frontier.*   Welland, Ont., 1896–1908.   9 vols.

———.   *Documents Relating to the Invasion of Canada and the Surrender of Detroit, 1812.*   Ottawa, 1913.

Duane, William L.   *The American Military Library: or Compendium of Modern Tactics.*   Philadelphia, 1809.   2 vols.

Fay, Herman A. (ed.). *Collection of the Official Accounts . . . of the Battles Between . . . the United States and Great Britain.* New York, 1817.

Furber, George C. *The Twelve Months Volunteer . . . Journal of a Private . . . in Mexico, 1846–1847.* Cincinnati, 1848.

Gleig, George R. *A Narrative of the British Campaign Against Washington, Baltimore, and New Orleans.* Philadelphia, 1821.

Glisan, Rodney. *Journal of Army Life [1855–1858].* San Francisco, 1874.

Henry, William S. *Campaign Sketches of the War with Mexico.* New York, 1847.

Hitchcock, Ethan A. *Fifty Years in Camp and Field.* Edited by W. A. Croffut. New York, 1909.

Hull, William. *Memoirs of the Campaign of the North Western Army of the United States, 1812.* Boston, 1824.

Kenley, John R. *Memoirs of a Maryland Volunteer in the War with Mexico.* Philadelphia, 1873.

Latour, A. Lacareiere. *Historical Memoirs of the War in West Florida and Louisiana in 1814–15.* Philadelphia, 1816.

Macomb, Alexander. *A Treatise on Martial Law and Courts-Martial; as Practiced in the United States of America.* Charleston, 1809.

Myers, William S. (ed.). *Mexican War Diary of George B. McClellan.* Princeton, 1917.

Nevins, Allan (ed.). *Polk, the Diary of a President.* New York, 1929.

Palmer, T. H. (ed.). *Historical Register of the United States (1812–1814).* Philadelphia, 1816. 4 vols.

Paullin, Charles O. (ed.). *The Battle of Lake Erie: a Collection of Documents.* Cleveland, 1918.

Pike, Zebulon M. *An Account of the Expedition of the Sources of the Mississippi . . . in the Years 1805, 1806, and 1807.* Philadelphia, 1810.

Prucha, Francis Paul. *Broadax and Bayonet.* State Historical Society of Wisconsin. 1953.

St. Clair, Arthur. *A Narrative . . . of the Campaign Against the Indians.* Philadelphia, 1812.

Scott, Winfield. *Memoirs.* New York, 1864. 2 vols.

Semmes, Raphael. *Service Afloat and Ashore During the Mexican War.* Cincinnati, 1851.

Smith, E. Kirby. *To Mexico with Scott.* Cambridge, Mass., 1917.

Taylor, Zachary. *Letters from the Battlefields of the Mexican War.* Rochester, N. Y., 1908.

Twitchell, Ralph E. *The History of the Military Occupation of the Territory of New Mexico from 1846 to 1851.* Denver, 1909.

U. S. Army (War Department). *Correspondence Between the Secretary of War and Generals Scott and Taylor.* Washington, 1848.

U. S. Navy. *Naval Documents Related to the Quasi-War Between the United States and France, 1797–1801.* Washington, 1935–38. 7 vols.

———. *Naval Documents Related to the United States War with the Barbary Powers, 1785–1807.* Washington, 1939–44. 6 vols.

Wilkinson, James. *Memoirs of My Own Times.* Philadelphia, 1816. 3 vols.

Wood, William C. H. *Select British Documents of the Canadian War of 1812.* Toronto, 1920–28. 4 vols.

Bibliographies

Bartlett, John R. (comp.).   *The Literature of the Rebellion, A Catalogue of Books and Pamphlets Relating to the Civil War* . . . .   Boston, 1866.

Freeman, Douglas S. (ed.).   *A Calendar of Confederate Papers with a Bibliography of some Confederate Publications.*   Richmond, 1908.

Freeman, Douglas S.   *The South to Posterity . . . Introduction to Confederate History.*   New York, 1939.

Nicholson, John P.   *Catalogue of Library of Brevet Lieutenant-Colonel John Page Nicholson . . . Relating to the War of the Rebellion, 1861–1866.*   Philadelphia, 1914.

U. S. Army (War Department).   *Bibliography of State Participation in the Civil War* . . . .   3d ed.; Washington, 1913.

General Works

Secondary Works

Adams, Ephraim D.   *Great Britain and the American Civil War.*   New York, 1925.   2 vols.

Bancroft, Frederic.   *William H. Seward.*   New York, 1900.   2 vols.

Bradford, Gamaliel.   *Confederate Portraits.*   Boston, 1914.

———.   *Union Portraits.*   Boston, 1916.

Capers, Henry D.   *The Life and Times of C. G. Memminger.*   Richmond, 1893.

Chadwick, French E.   *The Causes of the Civil War, 1859–1861.*   New York, 1906.

Craven, Avery O.   *The Coming of the Civil War.*   New York, 1942.

Dodd, William E.   *Lincoln or Lee* . . . .   New York, 1928.

Dyer, Frederick H. (comp.).   *A Compendium of the War of the Rebellion.*   Des Moines, 1908.

Eggleston, George C.   *The History of the Confederate War . . . A Narrative and Critical History.*   New York, 1910.   2 vols.

Fish, Carl R.   *The American Civil War.*   London and New York, 1937.

Gray, Wood.   *The Hidden Civil War: The Story of the Copperheads.*   New York, 1942.

Greeley, Horace.   *The American Conflict . . . 1860–64.*   Hartford, 1864–66.

Hendrick, Burton J.   *Lincoln's War Cabinet.*   Boston, 1946.

———.   *Statesmen of the Lost Cause.*   Boston, 1939.

Henry, Robert S.   *The Story of the Confederacy.*   Indianapolis, 1931.

Hesseltine, William B.   *Lincoln and the War Governors.*   New York, 1948.

Kirkland, Edward C.   *The Peacemakers of 1864.*   New York, 1927.

McElroy, Robert M.   *Jefferson Davis: the Unreal and the Real.*   New York, 1937.

Meade, Robert D. *Judah P. Benjamin, Confederate Statesman.* New York, 1943.

Miller, F. T. *Photographic History of the Civil War.* New York, 1911. 10 vols.

Milton, George F. *Conflict: The American Civil War.* New York, 1941.

Morrow, Curtis H. *Politico-Military Secret Societies of the Northwest, 1860–1865.* Worcester, 1929.

Nicolay, John G. and John Hay. *Abraham Lincoln: A History.* New York, 1890. 10 vols.

Oberholtzer, Ellis P. *Jay Cooke, Financier of the Civil War.* Philadelphia, 1907. 2 vols.

Owsley, Frank L. *King Cotton Diplomacy: Foreign Relations of the Confederate States.* . . . Chicago, 1931.

———. *States Rights in the Confederacy.* Chicago, 1931.

Paris, Louis P. (Comte de). *History of the Civil War in America.* Philadelphia, 1875–88. 4 vols.

Patrick, Rembert W. *Jefferson Davis and His Cabinet.* Baton Rouge, 1944.

Pratt, Fletcher. *Stanton: Lincoln's Secretary of War.* New York, 1953.

Randall, James G. *The Civil War and Reconstruction.* Boston, 1937.

———. *The Confiscation of Property during the Civil War.* . . . Indianapolis, 1913.

———. *Constitutional Problems under Lincoln.* New York, 1926.

———. *Lincoln the President.* . . . New York, 1945. 2 vols.

Rhodes, James F. *History of the Civil War, 1861–1865.* New York, 1917.

Schaff, Morris. *The Sunset of the Confederacy.* Boston, 1912.

Tatum, Georgia L. *Disloyalty in the Confederacy.* Chapel Hill, 1934.

Weeden, William B. *War Government, Federal and State, in Massachusetts, New York, Pennsylvania, and Indiana, 1861–1865.* Boston, 1906.

Wright, Edward N. *Conscientious Objectors in the Civil War.* . . . Philadelphia, 1931.

Printed Sources

Basler, Roy T. *Collective Works of Lincoln.* Rutgers, 1952.

Beale, Howard K. (ed.). *The Diary of Edward Bates, 1859–1866.* Washington, 1933.

Blackford, William W. *War Years with Jeb Stuart.* New York, 1945.

Borcke, Heros von. *Memoirs of the Confederate War for Independence.* Philadelphia, 1867; New York, 1938.

Chestnut, Mary B. *A Diary from Dixie.* Edited by Ben Ames Williams. Boston, 1949.

Davis, Jefferson. *The Rise and Fall of the Confederate Government.* New York, 1881. 2 vols.

Jones, John B. *A Rebel War Clerk's Diary.* . . . Philadelphia, 1866. 2 vols.

Moore, John B. (ed.). *The Works of James Buchanan, Comprising his Speeches, State Papers, and Private Correspondence.* Philadelphia, 1908–11. 12 vols.

Moore, Frank (ed.). *The Rebellion Record: A Diary of American Events, and Documents, Narratives, Illustrative Incidents, Poetry, etc.* New York, 1861–88. 12 vols.

Morse, John T., Jr. (ed.). *Diary of Gideon Wells.* . . . New York, 1911. 3 vols.

Nicolay, John G., and John Hay (eds.). *Abraham Lincoln: Complete Works.* New York, 1905. 12 vols.

Richardson, James D. *Messages and Papers of the Confederacy.* Nashville, 1905. 2 vols.

Rowland, Dunbar. *Jefferson Davis . . . His Letters, Papers, Speeches.* Jackson, Miss., 1923.

Russell, William H. *My Diary North and South.* Boston, 1863.

Special Military Works

Secondary Works

Adams, Charles F. *Lee at Appomattox, and Other Papers.* Boston, 1902.

Allen, William. *The Army of Northern Virginia in 1862.* Boston, 1892.

Anderson, Charles C. *Fighting by Southern Federals.* . . . New York, 1912.

Bache, Richard M. *Life of General George Gordon Meade, Commander of the Army of the Potomac.* Philadelphia, 1897.

Basso, Hamilton. *Beauregard: The Great Creole.* New York, 1933.

Baxter, James P. 3rd. *The Introduction of the Ironclad Warship.* Cambridge, Mass., 1933.

Benton, Josiah H. *Voting in the Field: A Forgotten Chapter of the Civil War.* Boston, 1915.

Bigelow, John. *Campaign of Chancellorsville.* . . . New Haven, 1910.

Black, Robert C. III. *The Railroads of the Confederacy.* Chapel Hill, 1952.

Bradford, Gamaliel. *Lee the American.* Boston, 1912.

Bradlee, Francis B. C. *Blockade Running during the Civil War.* . . . Salem, Mass., 1925.

Britton, Wiley. *The Civil War on the Border.* . . . New York, 1890–99. 2 vols.

Brown, D. Alexander. *Grierson's Raid.* Urbana, 1954.

Burne, Alfred H. *Lee, Grant, and Sherman, a Study in Leadership.* . . . Aldershot, England, 1938.

Catton, Bruce. *Mr. Lincoln's Army.* New York, 1949.

———. *Glory Road.* New York, 1952.

Cleaves, Freeman. *Rock of Chickamauga, the Life of General George H. Thomas.* Norman, Okla., 1948.

Conger, Arthur L. *The Rise of U. S. Grant.* New York, 1931.

Cox, Jacob D. *The Battle of Franklin, Tennessee, November 30, 1864.* New York, 1897.

———. *The March to the Sea: Franklin and Nashville.* New York, 1882.

Curtis, Newton M. *From Bull Run to Chancellorsville.* New York and London, 1906.

Denison, George T. *Soldiering in Canada.* Toronto, 1900.

Duke, Basil W. *Morgan's Cavalry.* New York, 1906.

Dunn, Jacob P. *History . . . Sioux War . . . Massacres . . . 1862 and 1863.* New York, 1864.

Dyer, John P. *"Fightin' Joe" Wheeler.* Baton Rouge, 1941.

Eckenrode, Hamilton J., and Bryan Conrad. *James Longstreet: Lee's War Horse.* Chapel Hill, 1935.

————. *George B. McClellan, the Man Who Saved the Union.* Chapel Hill, 1941.

Eliot, Ellsworth, Jr. *West Point in the Confederacy.* New York, 1941.

Fleming, Vivian M. *Campaigns of the Army of Northern Virginia . . . 1861–1865.* Richmond, 1928.

Flower, Frank A. *Edwin McMasters Stanton, the Autocrat of Rebellion, Emancipation and Reconstruction.* Akron, 1905.

Fox, William F. *Regimental Losses in the . . . Civil War.* Albany, 1889.

Freeman, Douglas S. *Lee's Lieutenants—A Study in Command.* New York, 1942–46. 3 vols.

————. *R. E. Lee, A Biography.* New York, 1934–35. 4 vols.

French, Samuel L. *The Army of the Potomac from 1861 to 1863 . . . .* New York, 1906.

Fry, James B. *New York and the Conscription of 1863. . . .* New York, 1885.

Fuller, Claud E., and Richard D. Steuart. *Firearms of the Confederacy.* . . . Huntington, W. Va., 1944.

Fuller, J. F. C. *Grant and Lee, a Study in Personality and Generalship.* New York, 1933.

————. *The Generalship of Ulysses S. Grant.* New York, 1929.

Gorham, George C. *Life and Public Service of Edwin M. Stanton.* Boston and New York, 1899. 2 vols.

Gordon, George. *Reminiscences of the Civil War.* New York, 1904.

Harrington, Fred H. *Fighting Politician: Maj. Gen. N. P. Banks.* Philadelphia, 1948.

Hay, Thomas R. *Hood's Tennessee Campaign.* New York, 1929.

Haydon, F. Stansbury. *Aeronautics in the Union and Confederate Armies . . . .* Baltimore, 1941.

Headley, John W. *Confederate Operations in Canada and New York.* New York, 1906.

Hebert, Walter H. *Fighting Joe Hooker.* Indianapolis, 1944.

Henderson, George F. R. *Stonewall Jackson and the . . . Civil War.* London, 1898. 2 vols.

Henry, Robert S. *"First with the Most" Forrest.* Indianapolis, 1944.

Hesseltine, William B. *Civil War Prisons: A Study in War Psychology.* Columbus, Ohio, 1930.

Horn, Stanley F. *The Army of Tennessee. . . .* Indianapolis, 1944.

Humphreys, Andrew A. *. . . The Virginia Campaign of '64 and '65. . . .* New York, 1883.

Huse, Caleb. *The Supplies for the Confederate Army: How They Were Obtained in Europe and How Paid For.* Boston, 1904.

Jones, Virgil C. *Ranger Mosby.* Chapel Hill, 1944.

Johnston, Robert M. *Bull Run: Its Strategy and Tactics.* Boston, 1913.

Johnston, William P. *The Life of Gen. Albert Sydney Johnston . . . .* New York, 1878.

Kearsey, Alexander H. C. *A Study . . . Strategy and Tactics . . . Shenandoah Valley Campaign, 1861-1862.* Aldershot, England, 1930.

Kellogg, Sanford C. *The Shenandoah Valley and Virginia, 1861 to 1865: A War Study.* New York, 1903.

Lee, Robert E. *Recollections and Letters of General Robert E. Lee, by His Son. . . .* Garden City, 1924.

Lewis, Lloyd. *Sherman—Fighting Prophet.* New York, 1932.

Liddell Hart, B. H. *Sherman: Soldier, Realist, American.* New York, 1929.

Livermore, Thomas L. *Numbers and Losses in the Civil War . . . 1861-1865.* Boston, 1900.

Longstreet, Helen D. *Lee and Longstreet at High Tide: Gettysburg in the Light of the Official Records.* Gainesville, Ga., 1904.

Lonn, Ella. *. . . Desertion during the Civil War.* New York, 1928.

Lytle, Andrew N. *Bedford Forrest and His Critter Company.* New York, 1931.

Macartney, Clarence E. N. *Lincoln and His Generals.* Philadelphia, 1925.

———. *Grant and His Generals.* New York, 1953.

Mahan, Alfred T. *. . . The Gulf and Inland Waters.* New York, 1883.

———. *Admiral Farragut.* New York, 1897.

Martin, Bessie. *Desertion of Alabama Troops from the Confederate Army: A Study in Sectionalism.* New York, 1932.

Maurice, Sir Frederick B. *Robert E. Lee, the Soldier.* Boston, 1925.

———. *Statesmen and Soldiers of the Civil War: A Study of the Conduct of the War.* Boston, 1926. (*Governments and War,* London, 1926.)

Meade, George. *The Life and Letters of General George Gordon Meade, Major-General United States Army.* New York, 1913. 2 vols.

Meneely, Alexander H. *The War Department in 1861. . . .* New York, 1928.

Michie, Peter S. *General McClellan.* New York, 1901.

Military Historical Society of Massachusetts. *Papers . . . .* Boston, 1881-1918. 14 vols.

Mitchell, Joseph B. *Decisive Battles of the Civil War.* New York, 1955.

Moore, Albert B. *Conscription and Conflict in the Confederacy.* New York, 1924.

Myers, William S. *A Study in Personality: General George Brinton McClellan.* New York, 1934.

O'Connor, Richard. *Hood: Cavalier General.* New York, 1949.

———. *Sheridan the Inevitable.* New York, 1953.

Pearson, Henry G. *James S. Wadsworth . . . Brevet Major General of United States Volunteers.* New York, 1913.

Pemberton, John. *General Pemberton, Defender of Vicksburg.* Chapel Hill, 1942.

Phisterer, Frederick. *Statistical Record of the Armies of the United States.* New York, 1883.

Poore, Benjamin P. *The Life . . . of Ambrose E. Burnside . . . .* Providence, 1882.

Porter, David D. *Naval History of the Civil War.* New York, 1886.

Pratt, Fletcher. *Stanton, Lincoln's Secretary of War.* New York, 1953.

Robinson, William M. *The Confederate Privateers.* New Haven, 1928.

Rhodes, Charles D. *History of the Cavalry of the Army of the Potomac.* Kansas City, Mo., 1900.

Ropes, John C., and William R. Livermore. *The Story of the Civil War . . . .* New York, 1894–1913. 3 vols.

Scharf, John T. *History of the Confederate States Navy . . . .* New York, 1887.

Seitz, Don Carlos. *Braxton Bragg.* Columbia, S. C., 1924.

Soley, James R. *The Blockade and the Cruisers.* New York, 1883.

Steele, Matthew F. *American Campaigns.* Washington, 1909. 2 vols.

Stickles, Arndt M. *Simon Boliver Buckner: Borderland Knight.* Chapel Hill, 1940.

Stillé, Charles J. *History of the United States Sanitary Commission . . . .* Philadelphia, 1866.

Stillwell, Leander. *The Story of a Common Soldier . . . in the Civil War.* Erie, Kans., 1917.

Taylor, Walter H. *General Lee, His Campaigns in Virginia, 1861–1865, with Personal Reminiscences.* Brooklyn, 1906.

Thomason, John W. Jr. *Jeb Stuart.* New York, 1930.

Vandiver, Frank E. *Ploughshares into Swords: Josiah Gorgas and Confederate Ordnance.* Boston, 1952.

Van Horne, Thomas B. *History of the Army of the Cumberland . . . .* Cincinnati, 1875.

———. *The Life of Major-General George H. Thomas.* New York, 1882.

Walker, Francis A. *General Hancock.* New York, 1894.

———. *History . . . Second Corps in . . . Army of the Potomac.* New York, 1886.

Weber, Thomas. *The Northern Railroads in the Civil War, 1861–1865.* New York, 1952.

Wiley, Bell I. *The Life of Billy Yank.* Indianapolis, 1952.

———. *The Life of Johnny Reb.* Indianapolis, 1943.

Williams, Kenneth P. *Lincoln Finds a General.* New York, 1949. 4 vols.

Williams, Thomas H. *Lincoln and His Generals.* New York, 1952.

Williamson, James J. *Mosby's Rangers. . . .* New York, 1896.

Wilson, James H. *The Life of John A. Rawlins. . . . Major General of Volunteers, and Secretary of War.* New York, 1916.

Wise, Jennings C. *The Long Arm of Lee: . . . History of the Artillery of the Army of Northern Virginia. . . .* Lynchburg, Va., 1915. 2 vols.

Wood, Walter B., and James E. Edmonds. *A History of the Civil War in the United States, 1861-1865.* London, 1905.

Wyeth, John A. *Life of General Nathan Bedford Forrest.* New York, 1899.

Printed Sources

Alexander, Edward P. *Military Memoirs of a Confederate . . . .* New York, 1907.

Butler, Benjamin F. *Autobiography . . . Benjamin F. Butler . . . .* Boston, 1892.

Commager, Henry S. (ed.). *The Blue and the Gray.* New York, 1950. 2 vols.

Cox, Jacob D. *Military Reminiscences of the Civil War.* New York, 1900. 2 vols.

Croffut, W. A. (ed.). *Fifty Years in Camp and Field, Diary of Major-General Ethan Allen Hitchcock, U.S.A.* New York, 1909.

Dana, Charles A. *Recollections of the Civil War.* New York, 1898.

Douglas, Henry K. *I Rode with Stonewall.* Chapel Hill, 1940.

Early, Jubal A. *Lieutenant General Jubal Anderson Early, C.S.A., Autobiographical Sketch . . . .* Philadelphia, 1912.

Fletcher, William A. *Rebel Private, Front and Rear . . . Through the Civil War.* Beaumont, Tex., 1908.

Ford, Worthington C. (ed.). *War Letters, 1862-1865, of John Chipman Gray and John Godman Ropes.* Boston, 1927.

Freeman, Douglas S. (ed). *Lee's Dispatches: Unpublished Letters of General Robert E. Lee, C.S.A., to Jefferson Davis and the War Department of the Confederate States of America, 1862-1865 . . . .* New York, 1915.

General Service Schools, Fort Leavenworth. *Fort Henry and Fort Donelson Campaigns: Source Book.* Fort Leavenworth, 1923.

———. *Source Book of the Peninsular Campaign in Virginia, April to July, 1862.* Fort Leavenworth, 1922.

Gibbon, John. *Personal Recollections of the Civil War.* New York, 1928.

Gordon, George H. *Brook Farm to Cedar Mountain.* Boston, 1883.

Grant, Ulysses S. *Personal Memoirs of U. S. Grant . . . .* New York, 1885–86. 2 vols.

Higginson, Thomas W. *Army Life in a Black Regiment.* Boston, 1870.

Hood, John B. *Advance and Retreat . . . .* New Orleans, 1880.

Howe, M. A. De Wolfe (ed.). *Marching with Sherman: Passages from the Letters and Campaign Diaries of Henry Hitchcock . . . .* New Haven, 1927.

Inman, Arthur C. (ed.). *Soldier of the South: General Pickett's War Letters to his Wife.* Cambridge, Mass., 1928.

Johnston, Joseph E. *Narrative of Military Operations . . . during the Late War Between the States.* New York, 1874.

Jones, Jenkin L. *An Artilleryman's Diary [1862-1865].* Madison, 1914.

Longstreet, James. *From Manassas to Appomattox: Memoirs of the Civil War in America.* Philadelphia, 1896.

Lyman, Theodore. *Meade's Headquarters, 1863–1865: Letters of Colonel Theodore Lyman from the Wilderness to Appomattox.* Edited by George R. Agassiz. Boston, 1922.

Marshall, Jessie A. (ed.). *Private and Official Correspondence of General Benjamin F. Butler during the Period of the Civil War.* Norwood, Mass., 1917. 5 vols.

Maurice, Sir Frederick B. (ed.). *An Aide-de-Camp of Lee, Being the Papers of Col. Charles Marshall . . . 1862–1865.* Boston, 1927.

McCarthy, Carlton. *Detailed Minutiae of Soldier Life . . . Army of Northern Virginia, 1861–1865.* Richmond, 1882.

McClellan, George B. *McClellan's Own Story . . . .* New York, 1887.

McKim, Randolph H. *A Soldier's Recollections . . . Diary of a Young Confederate . . . .* New York, 1910.

Merington, Marguerite (ed.). *The Custer Story.* New York, 1950.

Mosby, John S. *Memoirs.* Edited by Charles W. Russell. Boston, 1917.

Munson, John W. *Reminiscences of a Mosby Guerrilla.* New York, 1906.

Neese, George M. *Three Years in the Confederate Horse Artillery.* New York, 1911.

Porter, Horace. *Campaigning with Grant.* New York, 1897.

Schofield, John M. *Forty-Six Years in the Army.* New York, 1897.

Schurz, Carl. *The Reminiscences of Carl Schurz . . . .* New York, 1907–08. 3 vols.

Sheridan, Philip H. *Personal Memoirs of P. H. Sheridan . . . .* New York, 1888. 2 vols.

Sherman, William T. *Personal Memoirs of Gen. W. T. Sherman . . . .* New York, 1875–76–86–90–91. 2 vols.

Sorrel, G. Moxley. *Recollections of a Confederate Staff Officer.* New York, 1905.

Taylor, Richard. *Destruction & Reconstruction.* New York, 1879.

Thorndike, Rachel S. (ed.). *The Sherman Letters: Correspondence between General and Senator Sherman from 1837 to 1891.* New York, 1894.

Townsend, George A. *Rustics in Rebellion: A Yankee Reporter on the Road to Richmond, 1861–1865.* Durham, 1950.

U. S. Army (War Department). *Military Railroads 1861–1867.* (Undated compilation of General Orders, Instructions and Reports.)

———. *The War of the Rebellion: Official Records . . . .* Washington, 1880–1901. 130 vols. including 1 vol. of index and 3 vols. of atlases.

U. S. Congress—Senate. *Report of the Joint . . . Committee to Inquire into . . . Affairs in the Late Insurrectionary States.* Washington, 1872. 13 vols.

U. S. Navy (Navy Department). *The War of the Rebellion: Official Records . . . .* Washington, 1894–1922. 30 vols.

Vandiver, Frank E. (ed.). *The Civil War Diary of General Josiah Gorgas.* University, Ala., 1947.

Welles, Gideon. *Diary.* New York, 1911. 3 vols.

Wills, Charles W. *Army Life of an Illinois Soldier* . . . . Washington, 1906.

Wilson, James H. *Under the Old Flag: Recollections of Military Operations in the War for the Union, the Spanish War, the Boxer Rebellion* . . . . New York, 1912.

Section VII. SOURCE MATERIAL FOR THE WRITING OF AMERICAN MILITARY HISTORY: 1865–1898

Special Military Works

Secondary Works

Brady, Cyrus T. *Indian Fights and Fighters.* New York, 1916.

Downey, Fairfax D. *Indian Fighting Army.* New York, 1941.

Ellis, E. S. *The Indian Wars of the United States.* New York, 1892.

Grinnell, George B. *The Fighting Cheyennes.* New York, 1915.

Johnson, W. Fletcher. *The Life of Sitting Bull and the History of the Indian War, 1890–1891.* Philadelphia, 1891.

Kuhlman, Charles. *Legend into History.* Harrisburg, 1951.

Logan, John H. *The Volunteer Soldier of America.* Chicago and New York, 1887.

Luce, Edward S. *Keogh, Comanche, and Custer.* New York, 1939.

Wellman, Paul I. *Death on Horseback.* Philadelphia and New York, 1947.

Van De Water, Fredric F. *Glory Hunter: A Life of General Custer.* Indianapolis, 1934.

Printed Sources

Bourke, John G. *An Apache Campaign in the Sierra Madre.* New York, 1886.

———. *On the Border with Crook.* New York, 1891.

Brininstool, E. A. *A Trooper with Custer.* Columbus, 1925.

Crook, George. *Report of Operations Against the Apache Indians.* Cincinnati, 1885–86.

Custer, George A. *Wild Life on the Plains and Horrors of Indian Warfare.* St. Louis, 1891.

———. *My Life on the Plains.* New York, 1874.

Greely, Adolphus W. *Three Years of Arctic Service.* New York, 1886.

Howard, Oliver O. *My Life and Experiences Among our Hostile Indians.* Hartford, 1907.

———. *Chief Joseph . . . His Pursuit and Capture.* Boston, 1881.

King, Charles. *Campaigns with Crook and Stories of Army Life.* New York, 1905.

McCall, George A. *Letters from the Frontiers.* Philadelphia, 1868.

Miles, Nelson A. *Personal Recollections.* Chicago, 1896.

SPANISH-AMERICAN WAR—PHILIPPINE INSURRECTION—CHINA RELIEF EXPEDITION

General Works

Secondary Works

Chadwick, French E.   *The Relations of the United States and Spain- -The Spanish-American War*.   New York, 1909.   2 vols.

Clements, Paul H.   *The Boxer Rebellion: A Political and Diplomatic Review*. New York, 1915.

Elliott, Charles B.   *The Philippines*.   Indianapolis, 1917.   2 vols.

Millis, Walter.   *The Martial Spirit: A Study of our War with Spain*.   Cambridge, 1931.

Pratt, Julius W.   *Expansionists of 1898*.   Baltimore, 1936.

Root, Elihu.   *The Military and Colonial Policy of the United States*.   Cambridge, 1916.

Special Military Works

Secondary Works

Blount, James H.   *The American Occupation of the Philippines, 1898–1912*. New York, 1912.

Carter, William H.   *The Life of Lieutenant General Chaffee*.   Chicago, 1917.

Davis, Richard H.   *Cuban and Porto Rican Campaigns*.   New York, 1898.

Harper's Pictorial History of the War with Spain.   New York, 1899.   2 vols.

Healy, Laurin H. and Luis Kutner.   *The Admiral*.   New York, 1944.

LeRoy, James A.   *The Americans in the Philippines*.   New York, 1914.   2 vols.

Mahan, Alfred T.   *Lessons of the War with Spain*.   Boston, 1898.

Pringle, Henry F.   *The Life and Times of William Howard Taft*.   New York and Toronto, 1939.

Sargent, Herbert H.   *The Campaign of Santiago de Cuba*.   Chicago, 1907.

Sargent, Nathan.   *Admiral Dewey and the Manila Campaign*.   Washington, 1947.

Sexton, William T.   *Soldiers in the Philippines: A History of the Insurrection*. Washington, 1944.   (Originally published as *Soldiers in the Sun*. Harrisburg, 1939.)

Storey, Moorfield, and Marcial P. Lichauco.   *The Conquest of the Philippines by the United States, 1898–1925*.   New York, 1926.

Titherington, Richard H.   *A History of the Spanish-American War of 1898*. New York, 1900.

Waite, Carleton Frederick.   *Some elements of International Military Cooperation in the Suppression of the 1900 Antiforeign Rising in China with Special Reference to the Forces of the United States*.   Los Angeles, 1935.

West, Richard S.   *Admirals of American Empire*.   New York, 1948.

Wilkerson, Marcus M. *Public Opinion and the Spanish-American War.*
Baton Rouge, 1932.
Wilson, Herbert W. *The Downfall of Spain: Naval History of the Spanish-American War.* London, 1900.

Printed Sources

Alger, Russell A. *The Spanish-American War.* New York, 1901.
Daggett, Aaron S. *America in the China Relief Expedition.* Kansas City, 1903.
Dewey, George. *Autobiography of George Dewey.* New York, 1913.
Funston, Frederick. *Memories of Two Wars.* New York, 1911.
Goode, W. A. M. *With Sampson Though the War.* New York, 1899.
Long, John D. *The New American Navy.* New York, 1903.
Miles, Nelson A. *Serving the Republic.* New York, 1911.
Miley, John D. *In Cuba with Shafter.* New York, 1899.
Millet, Frank D. *The Expedition to the Philippines.* New York, 1899.
Roosevelt, Theodore. *The Rough Riders.* New York, 1899.
Schley, Winfield S. *Forty-Five Years Under the Flag.* New York, 1904.
U. S. Army (War Department):
  Adjutant General's Office. *Correspondence Relating to the War with Spain . . . the Insurrection in the Philippines and the China Relief Expedition.* Washington, 1902. 2 vols.
  Reports on Military Operations in South Africa and China. Washington, 1901.
  Statistical Exhibit of Strength of Volunteer Forces Called into Service During the War with Spain with Losses from all Causes. Washington, 1899.
U. S. Congress—Senate:
  Food Furnished by Subsistence Department to Troops in the Field. (Doc. No. 270, 56th Cong., 1st sess.) Washington, 1900. 3 vols.
  Report of the Commission Appointed by the President to Investigate the Conduct of the War Department in the War with Spain. (Doc. No. 221, 56th Cong., 1st sess. Commonly known as the Dodge Report.) Washington, 1900. 8 vols.
U. S. Navy (Navy Department). Office of Naval Intelligence. *Notes on the Spanish-American War.* Washington, 1900.
Wagner, Arthur L. *Report of the Santiago Campaign 1898.* Kansas City, 1908.
Wheeler, Joseph. *The Santiago Campaign 1898.* Boston, 1898.

Section IX. SOURCE MATERIAL FOR THE WRITING OF AMERICAN MILITARY HISTORY: 1903–1919

Bibliographies

Cru, Jean Norton. *Témoins—Essais d'Analyse et de Critique des Souvenirs Combattants.* Paris 1915–28.
Falls, Cyril B. *War Books—A Critical Guide.* London, 1930.
French Historical Section. *Bibliographies on the World War, 1914–1918.*

390016 O - 56 - 10

Frothingham, Thomas G. *Guide to the Military History of the World War.* Boston, 1920.

Green, Robert C. "Selected Bibliography of the European War 1914–18." Unpublished manuscript, National War College Library, 1934.

Kunz, Josef Laurenz. *Bibliographie der Kriegsliteratur.* Berlin, 1920.

Leland, Waldo G. and Newton D. Mereness. *Introduction to the American Official Sources for the Economic and Social History of the World War.* New Haven, 1926.

Prothero, Sir George W., K. B. E. *A Selected Analytical List of Books Concerning the Great War.* London, 1923.

General Works

Secondary Works

Angell, Norman. *The Great Illusion.* New York, 1933.

Aston, George G. *The Great War of 1914–1918.* London, 1930.

Baker, Ray S. *Life and Letters of Woodrow Wilson.* New York, 1935.

Clarkson, Grosvenor B. *Industrial America in the World War.* Cambridge, 1923.

Cruttwell, Charles R. M. F. *A History of the Great War, 1914–1918.* Oxford, 1934.

Du Val, Miles P., Jr., *Cadiz to Cathay.* Palo Alto, 1940.

———. *And the Mountains Will Move.* Palo Alto, 1947.

Edmonds, James E. *A Short History of the World War I.* London, 1951.

Fay, Sidney B. *The Origins of the World War.* New York, 1930. 2 vols.

Gooch, G. P. *Before the War.* New York, 1936. 2 vols.

Mansergh, N. *The Coming of the First World War.* New York and London, 1949.

Millis, Walter. *The Road to War, America, 1914–1917.* Boston and New York, 1935.

Moore, Samuel T. *America and the World War . . . .* New York, 1937.

Seymour, Charles. *American Diplomacy During the World War.* Baltimore, 1934.

———. *American Neutrality, 1914–1917.* New Haven, 1935.

———. *Woodrow Wilson and the World War.* New Haven, 1931.

Squires, J. Duane. *British Propaganda at Home and in the United States from 1914 to 1917.* Cambridge, 1935.

Tansill, Charles C. *America Goes to War.* Boston, 1938.

Printed Sources

Bernstorff, J. C. von. *My Three Years in America.* New York, 1920.

Special Military Works

Secondary Works

American Battle Monuments Commission. *A Guide to the American Battlefields of Europe.* Washington, 1927.

Ayres, Leonard P. *The War with Germany, a Statistical Summary.* Washington, 1919.

Baruch, Bernard M. *American Industry in War.* New York, 1941.

Buchan, John. *A History of the Great War.* London and New York, 1921–22. 4 vols.

Chambrun, J. A. de. *The American Army in the European Conflict.* New York, 1919.

Clinard, O. J. *Japan's Influence on American Naval Power, 1897–1919.* Berkeley, 1947.

Cunee, John. *The Air Weapons 1914–1916.* Harrisburg, 1947.

Dickinson, John. *The Building of an Army.* New York, 1922.

Edmonds, James E. *Military Operations, France and Belgium, 1918.* London, 1935.

Frothingham, Thomas G. *American Reinforcements in the World War.* New York, 1928.

————. *The Naval History of the World War . . . .* Cambridge, 1924–26. 3 vols.

German Reichsarchiv. *Der Weltkrieg, 1914–1918.* Berlin, 1925–39. 14 vols.

Great Britain Committee of Imperial Defense. *History of the Great War.* London, 1920–49. 50 vols. and maps.

Hagedorn, Hermann. *Leonard Wood, A Biography.* New York and London, 1931.

Hines, Walter D. *War History of American Railroads.* New Haven, 1928.

Huidekoper, Frederic L. *Military Unpreparedness of the United States.* New York, 1915.

Infantry School. *Infantry in Battle.* Washington, 1934.

Jessup, Philip. *Elihu Root.* New York, 1938. 2 vols.

Johnson, Douglas W. *Battlefields of the World War.* Greenwich, 1921. 2 vols., 1 of text and 1 of maps.

Johnson, Thomas M. *Without Censor.* Indianapolis, 1928.

Kittredge, Tracy B. *Naval Lessons of the Great War.* Garden City, 1921.

Lockmiller, David A. *Magoon in Cuba—A Brief History of the Second Intervention, 1906–1909.* Chapel Hill, 1938.

Lucas. (Given name unknown) *The Evolution of Tactical Ideas in France and Germany During the War of 1914–1918.* MS translation by P. V. Kieffer, Army War College, 1925. Paris, 1924.

Maurice, Sir Frederick. *Lessons of Allied Co-operation: Naval, Military and Air 1914–1918.* London, New York, Toronto, 1942.

Ministère de la Guerre, Etat-Major de l'Armée, Service Historique. *Les Armées Francaises dans la Grande Guerre.* Paris, 1922–38. 11 tomes, 64 vols.

Mock, James R. *Censorship.* Princeton, 1941.

Mock, James R., and Cedric Larson. *Words that Won the War.* Princeton, 1939.

Nicolai, W. *The German Secret Service.* London, 1924.

Padelford, Norman J. *The Panama Canal in Peace and War.* New York, 1942.

Palmer, Frederick C. *Newton D. Baker, America at War.* New York, 1931. 2 vols.

————. *Bliss, Peacemaker, The Life and Letters of Gen. Tasker H. Bliss.* New York, 1934.

————. *John J. Pershing, General of the Armies.* Harrisburg, 1948.

Paxson, Frederick L. *American Democracy and the World War.* Boston, 1936–48. 3 vols.

Peterson, Horace C. *Propaganda for War, the Campaign Against American Neutrality, 1914–1917.* Norman, Okla., 1939.

Pringle, Henry F. *Life and Times of Wm. Howard Taft.* New York, 1939. 2 vols.

————. *Theodore Roosevelt, A Biography.* New York, 1931.

Read, James M. *Atrocity Propaganda, 1914–1919.* New Haven, London, 1941.

Sprout, Harold and Margaret. *Toward a New Order of Sea Power: American Naval Policy and the World Scene.* Princeton, 1943.

————. *The Rise of American Naval Power.* Princeton, 1939.

Strakovsky, Leonid I. *The Origin of American Intervention in North Russia.* Princeton, 1937.

Sweetser, A. W. *The American Air Service.* New York, 1919.

U. S. Army. The Surgeon General. *Medical Department of the Army in World War.* Washington, 1925–29. 15 vols.

Viereck, George S. *Spreading Germs of Hate.* New York, 1930.

White, John A. *The Siberian Intervention.* Princeton, 1950.

Wilgus, William. *Transporting the A.E.F. in Western Europe.* New York, 1931.

Printed Sources

Allen, Henry T. *The Rhineland Occupation.* Indianapolis, 1927.

Bullard, Robert L. *Personalities and Reminiscences.* New York, 1925.

Carter, William H. *Creation of the American General Staff.* (S. Doc. No. 119, 68th Cong., 1st sess.) Washington, 1924.

Creel, George. *How We Advertised America . . . .* New York and London, 1920.

Crowell, Benedict. *America's Munitions, 1917–1918.* Washington, 1919.

Dawes, Charles G. *Journal of the Great War.* Boston, 1921. 2 vols.

————. *Report of the Board of Military Supply.* France, England, Washington, 1924. 2 vols.

Dickman, Joseph T. *The Great Crusade.* New York, 1925.

Gorgas, William C. *Sanitation in Panama.* New York and London, 1928.

Graves, William S. *America's Siberian Adventure 1918–1920.* New York, 1931.

Great Britain War Office. *Statistics of the Military Effort of the British Empire during the Great War, 1914–1920.* London, 1922.

Hagood, Johnson. *The Services of Supply.* Boston, 1927.

Haig, Sir Douglas. *Despatches (December 1915–April 1919).* London and Toronto; New York, 1935. 2 vols.

Harbord, James A. *American Army in France.* Boston, 1936.

————. *Leaves from a War Diary.* New York, 1925.

————. *America in the World War.* Boston and New York, 1933.

Hurley, Edward N. *The Bridge to France.* Philadelphia, 1927.

Lejeune, John A. *The Reminiscences of a Marine.* Philadelphia, 1930.

Liggett, Hunter. *Commanding an American Army—Recollections of the World War.* Boston, 1925.

———. *Ten Years Ago in France.* New York, 1928.

March, Peyton C. *The Nation at War.* New York, 1932.

McBride, Herbert W. *A Rifleman Went to War.* Marines, N. C., 1935.

Mitchell, William. *Our Air Force—The Keystone of National Defense.* New York, 1921.

———. *Winged Defense: The Development and Possibilities of Modern Air Power—Economic and Military.* New York and London, 1925.

Patrick, M. M. *The United States in the Air.* New York, 1928.

Pershing, John J. *My Experiences in the World War.* New York, 1931.

———. *Final Report, American Expeditionary Forces.* Washington, 1920.

Scott, Hugh L. *Some Memories of a Soldier.* New York, 1928.

Seymour, Charles (ed.). *Intimate Papers of Col. House.* Boston and New York, 1930. 4 vols.

Sims, William S., and Burton J. Hendrick. *The Victory at Sea.* New York, 1920.

Thomason, John W. Jr. *Fix Bayonets.* New York, 1927.

Tompkins, Frank. *Chasing Villa.* Harrisburg, n. d.

U. S. Army:

Chief of Engineers. *Historical Report of the Chief Engineer, A.E.F.* Washington, 1919.

War Department:

Order of Battle of the U. S. Land Forces in the World War, A.E.F. . . . Washington, 1937.

Order of Battle of the U. S. Land Forces in the World War, A.E.F. Divisions. Washington, 1931.

Order of Battle of the U. S. Land Forces in the World War, Zone of the Interior. Washington, 1949.

Order of Battle of the U. S. Land Forces in the World War, Zone of the Interior—Directory of Troops. Washington, 1949.

Genesis of the American First Army. Washington, 1938.

A Study in Troop Frontage. Washington, 1920.

Organization of the Services of Supply, A.E.F. Washington, 1921.

Blanc Mont. Washington, 1922.

Operations of the 2d American Corps in Somme Offensive. Washington, 1920.

U. S. Army in the World War 1917-1919 (Documentary History). Washington, 1948. 17 vols.

Handbook of Economic Agencies in the War of 1917. Washington, 1919.

White, John R. *Bullets and Bolos.* New York, 1928.

Section X. SOURCE MATERIAL FOR THE WRITING OF AMERICAN MILITARY HISTORY: 1919–1947

Bibliographies

Inventory of the Records of Office of Civilian Defense. Washington, 1945. 2 vols.

Office of the Chief of Military History. *Unit Histories of World War II.* Washington, 1950.

Taylor, Philip H. and Ralph J. D. Braibanti. *Administration of Occupied Areas.* Syracuse, 1948.

U. S. Board of Economic Warfare. *Bibliography of Military Occupation.* Washington, 1942.

General Works

Secondary Works

Beard, Charles A. *President Roosevelt and the Coming of the War 1941.* New Haven, 1948.

Elliott, William Y. *Mobilization Planning and the National Security.* Washington, 1950.

Haines, Charles G., and Ross J. Hoffman. *Origins and Background of the Second World War.* London and New York, 1943.

Huzar, Elias. *The Purse and the Sword, 1918-1950.* Ithaca, 1950.

Langer, William L. and S. Everett Gleeson. *The Undeclared War.* New York, 1954.

Novick, David, Melvin Anshen, and W. C. Truppner. *Wartime Production Controls.* New York, 1949.

Rauch, Basil. *Roosevelt: From Munich to Pearl Harbor.* New York, 1950.

Royal Institute of International Affairs. *Chronology of the Second World War.* London, 1947.

Sherwood, Robert E. *Roosevelt and Hopkins: An Intimate History.* New York, 1948.

Somers, Herman M. *Presidential Agency: Office of War Mobilization and Reconversion.* Cambridge, 1950.

Spykman, Nicholas J. *The Geography of the Peace.* Edited by Helen R. Nicholl. New York, 1944.

Tansill, George C. *Backdoor to War.* Chicago, 1952.

United States Civilian Production Administration. *Industrial Mobilization for War.* Washington, 1947.

Printed Sources

The War Reports. Philadelphia, 1947.

Toynbee, Arnold (ed.). *Documents on International Affairs 1939-1946,* vol. 1: March–September 1939. (Issued under the auspices of the Royal Institute of International Affairs.) London, 1951.

U. S. Congress. *Hearings Before the Joint Committee on the Investigation of the Pearl Harbor Attack.* 79th Cong., 1st sess. Washington, 1946. 39 vols.

Special Military Works

Secondary Works

Army Air Forces Aid Society. *Official Pictorial History of the AAF.* Washington, 1947.

Arnold and Eaker. *Winged Warfare.* New York and London, 1941.

Baldwin, Hanson W. *Great Mistakes of the War.* New York, 1950.

Cant, Gilbert. *The Great Pacific Victory from the Solomons to Tokyo.* New York, 1946.

Cirne Crance, J. de M. *The United States Marines: A Pictorial History.* New Orleans, 1952.

Dziuban, Col. Stanley W. Ms "United States Military Cooperation with Canada in World War II." Office, Chief of Military History. Washington, 1954.

Edmonds, Walter. *They Fought with What They Had.* Boston, 1951.

Frank, A., and J. D. Horan. *U.S.S. Seawolf.* New York, 1945.

Friedmann, Wolfgang. *The Allied Military Government of Germany.* London, 1947.

Friedrich, C. H., and Associates. *American Experiences in Military Government in World War II.* New York, 1948.

Fuller, J. F. C. *The Second World War 1939-45.* London, 1948.

Geer, Andrew. *The New Breed.* New York, 1952.

Hinton, Harold. *Air Victory.* New York, 1948.

Isely, Jeter A., and Philip A. Crowl. *The U. S. Marines and Amphibious War: Its Theory, and Its Practice in the Pacific.* Princeton, 1951.

Karig, Walter, and Others. *Battle Report:*
    Vol. I: *Pearl Harbor to Coral Sea.* New York, 1944.
    Vol. II: *The Atlantic War.* New York, 1946.
    Vol. III: *Pacific War—Middle Phase.* New York, 1947.
    Vol. IV: *The End of an Empire.* New York, 1948.
    Vol. V: *Victory in the Pacific.* New York, 1949.

King, Ernest J., and Walter Muir. *Fleet Admiral King: A Naval Record.* New York, 1952.

Liddell Hart, B. H. *Defence of the West.* New York, 1950.

Marshal, Samuel L. A. *Men Against Fire.* Washington, 1947.

McInnis, Edgar. *The War* .... Toronto, 1940–46. 6 vols.

McMillan, George. *The Old Breed: A History of the First Marine Division in World War II.* Washington, 1949.

Pollock, J. *Germany Under Occupation.* 2d ed.; Ann Arbor, 1947.

Pratt, Fletcher. *Fleet Against Japan.* New York, 1946.

Sherrod, Robert. *History of Marine Corps Aviation in World War II.* Washington, 1952.

Social Science Research Council. *Studies in Social Psychology in World War II.* Princeton, 1949–50. 4 vols.

Stockman, James R. *The Battle for Tarawa.* Washington, 1947.

Theodore, Roscoe. *United States Operations in World War II.* Annapolis, 1949.

U. S. Army (War Department):
    Quartermaster Corps Historical Studies. Washington, 1943–48. Consisting of 19 studies of activities pertaining to the Quartermaster Corps.
    Handbook on German Military Forces. TM–E 30–451. Washington, 1946.
    United States Army in World War II.
    Appleman, Roy E., and Others. *Okinawa: The Last Battle.* Washington, 1947.

Cannon, M. Hamlin. *Leyte: Return to the Philippines.* Washington, 1954.

Cline, Ray S. *Washington Command Post: The Operations Division.* Washington, 1951.

Cole, Hugh M. *The Lorraine Campaign.* Washington, 1950.

Crowl, Philip A. and Edmund G. Love. *The Seizure of the Gilberts and Marshalls.* Washington, 1955.

Green, Constance, and Others. *The Ordnance Department: Planning Munitions for War.* Washington, 1955.

Greenfield, Kent R., and Others. *The Organization of Ground Combat Troops.* Washington, 1947.

Harrison, Gordon A. *Cross Channel Attack.* Washington, 1951.

Howe, George F. *Operations in Northwest Africa, 1941-43.* Washington, 1956.

Kieffer, Chester L., and Erna Risch. *Quartermaster Corps: Organization, Supply and Services: Zone of Interior.* Vol. II. Washington, 1955.

Larson, Harold and Joseph Bykofsky. *The Transportation Corps: Operations Overseas.* Washington, 1956.

Leighton, Richard M. and Others. *Global Logistics and Strategy: 1940-1943.* Washington, 1955.

MacDonald, Charles B., and S. T. Mathews. *Three Battles: Arnaville, Altuzzo, and Schmidt.* Washington, 1952.

Miller, John, Jr. *Guadalcanal: The First Offensive.* Washington, 1949.

Millett, John. *The Organization and Role of the Army Service Forces.* Washington, 1954.

Morton, Louis. *Fall of the Philippines.* Washington, 1953.

Motter, T. H. Vail. *Persian Corridor and Aid to Russia.* Washington, 1952.

Palmer, Robert R., and Others. *The Procurement and Training of Ground Combat Troops.* Washington, 1948.

Pictorial Record: The War Against Germany and Italy: The Mediterranean and Adjacent Areas. Washington, 1951.

Pictorial Record: The War Against Germany: Europe and Adjacent Areas. Washington, 1951.

Pictorial Record: The War Against Japan. Washington, 1951.

Pogue, Forrest C. *The Supreme Command.* Washington, 1954.

Risch, Erna. *Quartermaster Corps: Organization, Supply and Services: Zone of Interior.* Vol. I. Washington, 1953.

Romanus, Charles F., and Riley Sunderland. *Stilwell's Mission to China.* Washington, 1953.

———. *Stilwell's Command Problems.* Washington, 1956.

Ruppenthal, Roland G. *Logistical Support of Armies—I.* Washington, 1954.

Smith, Robert R. *Approach to the Philippines.* Washington, 1953.

Snell, Edwin M. and Maurice Matloff. *Strategic Planning for Coalition Warfare.* Washington, 1953.

Stauffer, Alvin P. *The Quartermaster Corps: Operations in the War Against Japan.* Washington, 1956.

Terrett, Delaney. *The Signal Corps: The Emergency* (to December 1941). Washington, 1956.

———. *The Signal Corps: The Test* (December 1941 to July 1943). Washington, 1956.

Treadwell, Mattie. *The Women's Army Corps.* Washington, 1954.

Wardlow, Chester C. *Transportation Corps: Responsibilities, Organization and Operations.* Washington, 1952.

———. *The Transportation Corps: Movements, Training and Supply.* Washington, 1956.

Watson, Mark S. *Chief of Staff: Prewar Plans and Preparations.* Washington, 1950.

United States Army Air Forces in World War II:

Craven, Wesley F., and James L. Cate. *Plans and Early Operations.* Chicago, 1948.

———. *Europe: TORCH TO POINTBLANK.* Chicago, 1949.

———. *Europe: ARGUMENT to VE Day.* Chicago, 1951.

———. *Pacific: Guadalcanal to Saipan.* Chicago, 1950.

———. *Pacific: Matterhorn to Nagasaki.* Chicago, 1953.

———. *Men and Planes.* Chicago, 1954.

United States Military Academy. Stamps, T. D., and Vincent J. Esposito. *The Military History of World War II.* West Point, 1953, 2 vols.

United States Naval Operations in World War II:

Morison, Samuel E. *The Battle of the Atlantic September 1939–May 1943.* Boston, 1947.

———. *Operations in North African Waters October 1942–June 1943.* Boston, 1947.

———. *The Rising Sun in the Pacific 1931–April 1942.* Boston, 1948.

———. *Coral Sea, Midway and Submarine Actions May 1942–August 1942.* Boston 1949.

———. *The Struggle for Guadalcanal August 1942–February 1943.* Boston, 1949.

———. *Breaking the Bismarcks Barrier, 22 July 1942–1 May 1944.* Boston, 1950.

———. *Conquest of Micronesia.* Boston, 1951.

———. *Aleutians, Gilberts and Marshalls: June 1942–April 1944.* Boston, 1951.

———. *New Guinea and the Mariannas, March 1944–August 1944.* Boston, 1953.

———. *Sicily, Salerno, Anzio.* Boston, 1954.

Willoughby, Charles A. and John Chamberlain. *MacArthur 1941–1951.* New York, 1954.

Wilmot, Chester. *The Struggle for Europe.* New York, 1952.

Zink, Harold. *American Military Government in Germany.* New York, 1947.

Printed Sources

Arnold, Henry H. *Global Mission.* New York, 1949.

Baxter, James P. *Scientists Against Time.* Boston, 1946.

Bradley, Omar. *A Soldier's Story.* New York, 1951.

Brereton, Louis H. *The Brereton Diaries.* New York, 1946.

Chennault, Claire. *Way of a Fighter.* New York, 1949.

Clark, Mark W. *Calculated Risk.* New York, 1950.

Clay, Lucius. *Decision in Germany.* New York, 1950.

Deane, John R. *The Strange Alliance.* New York, 1947.

De Lattre. *Histoire De La Premiere Armée Francaise.* Paris, 1949.

Eichelberger, Robert L. *Our Jungle Road to Tokyo.* New York, 1950.

Eisenhower, Dwight D. *Crusade in Europe.* New York, 1948.

Halsey, William S., and J. Bryan, 3d. *Admiral Halsey's Story.* New York, 1947.

Kenney, George C. *General Kenney Reports.* New York, 1949.

King, E. J. *United States Navy at War, 1941–1945.* Washington, 1946. Admiral King's reports to Secretary of the Navy.

Krueger, Walter. *From Down Under to Nippon.* .Washington, 1953.

Leahy, William D. *I Was There.* New York, 1950.

MacDonald, Charles B. *Company Commander.* Washington, 1947.

Morgan, Sir Frederick. *Overture to Overlord.* Garden City, 1950.

Nelson, Donald M. *Arsenal of Democracy.* New York, 1946.

Patton, George S. Jr. *War as I Knew It.* Boston, 1947.

Sherman, Frederick C. *Combat Command: The American Aircraft Carriers in the Pacific War.* New York, 1950.

Smyth, Henry D. *Atomic Energy for Military Purposes; the Official Report on the Development of the Atomic Bomb under the Auspices of the United States Government 1940–45.* Princeton, 1946.

Stettinius, Edward R. Jr. *Lend-Lease: Weapon for Victory.* New York, 1944.

———. *Roosevelt and the Russians—the Yalta Conference.* Edited by Walter Johnson. Garden City, 1949.

Stilwell, Joseph W. *Papers.* Arranged and edited by Theodore H. White. New York, 1948.

Stimson, Henry L., and McGeorge Bundy. *On Active Service in Peace and War.* New York, 1948.

Truscott, Lucian K. *Command Missions, A Personal Story.* New York, 1954.

U. S. Government. National Archives. *Federal Records of World War II.* Washington, 1951. Vol. II: Military agencies.

Wainwright, Jonathan M. *General Wainwright's Story.* New York, 1946.

Section XI. SOURCE MATERIAL FOR THE WRITING OF AMERICAN MILITARY HISTORY: 1947–1954

Special Military Works

Secondary Works

Meade, E. Grant. *American Military Government in Korea.* New York, 1951.

Poats, Rutherford M. *Decisions in Korea.* New York, 1954.

Sawyer, Robert K. "United States Military Advisory Group to the Republic of Korea." Washington, 1955.

Thomas, R. C. W. *The War in Korea 1950–1953*. Aldershot, England, 1954.

U. S. Army, Office of the Chief of Military History:

Appleman, Roy E. *Combat Operations in Korea, June 1950–November 1950*. Washington, 1956.

Gugeler, Russell A. *Combat Actions in Korea: Infantry, Artillery, Armor*. Washington, 1954.

Pictorial Volumes:

Korea: 1950. Washington, 1952.

Korea: 1951–1953. Washington, 1956.

Westover, John G. *Combat Support in Korea*. Washington, 1955.

U. S. Marine Corps: Marine Operations in Korea, 1950–1953.

Montross, L. and N. A. Canzona. *Pusan Perimeter*. Washington, 1955.

U. S. Navy:

Karig, Walter, and Others. *Battle Report*. Vol. VI: *The War in Korea*. New York, 1952.

Willoughby, Charles A. and John Chamberlain. *MacArthur 1941–1951*. New York, 1954.

Printed Sources

Clark, Mark W. *From the Danube to the Yalu*. New York, 1954.

INDEX

145